TORPEDOED!

TORPEDOED!

A World War II Story of a Sinking Passenger
Ship and Two Children's Survival at Sea

CHERYL MULLENBACH

CHICAGO
REVIEW
PRESS

Copyright © 2017 by Cheryl Mullenbach
All rights reserved
First hardcover edition published 2017
First paperback edition published 2022
Published by Chicago Review Press Incorporated
814 North Franklin Street
Chicago, Illinois 60610
ISBN 978-1-64160-572-4

The Library of Congress has cataloged the hardcover edition as follows:
Names: Mullenbach, Cheryl, author.
Title: Torpedoed! : a World War II story of a sinking passenger ship and two
   children's survival at sea / Cheryl Mullenbach.
Other titles: World War II story of a sinking passenger ship and two
   children's survival at sea
Description: Chicago, Illinois : Chicago Review Press Incorporated, [2017] |
   Includes bibliographical references and index. | Audience: Age 10.
Identifiers: LCCN 2017000468 (print) | LCCN 2017000893 (ebook) | ISBN
   9781613738245 (cloth) | ISBN 9781613738252 (Pdf) | ISBN 9781613738276
   (Epub) | ISBN 9781613738269 (Kindle)
Subjects: LCSH: Athenia (Steamship)—Juvenile literature. | World War, 1939–1945—
   Naval operations, German—Juvenile literature. | World War, 1939–1945—Naval
   operations—Submarine—Juvenile literature. | World War, 1939–1945—Children—
   United States—Juvenile literature. | Kelley, Florence, 1925—Childhood and youth—
   Juvenile literature. | Park, Russell A., 1928–1996—Childhood and youth—Juvenile
   literature. | Shipwrecks—North Atlantic Ocean—Juvenile literature. | Shipwreck
   survival—Juvenile literature. | Passenger ships—Great Britain—History—20th
   century—Juvenile literature. | Children and war—United States—Juvenile
   literature.
Classification: LCC D772.A7 M85 2017 (print) | LCC D772.A7 (ebook) | DDC
   940.54/293—dc23
LC record available at https://lccn.loc.gov/2017000468

Cover design: Jonathan Hahn
Cover illustration: Marnie Galloway
Interior design: Sarah Olson
Map design: Chris Erichsen

Printed in the United States of America

~~~~~

Always for Ralph and Zola Mullenbach
And
Richard L. Wohlgamuth
Also for
Verlyn, Sue, Cory, Lindsey, Dan, Kelly, Curt, Sandy,
Kristie, Jeff, Troy, Tami, Danielle, Matt, and Jake

~~~~~

CONTENTS

~~~

PROLOGUE

As I looked forward, I saw a hatch and two people had been sitting on it. They were blown up into the air and back down onto the deck . . . very lifeless.

—Florence Kelly Roseman, 2010

At the time of her sinking, it is claimed, there were no living persons left on board the Athenia.

—Russell A. Park, 1989

People who lived to talk about it described horrific scenes of dazed kids sobbing for missing parents, burned men moaning in agony, and, worst of all, lifeless, broken bodies scattered across the decks. Passengers on the liner *Athenia* traveling through the dangerous waters of the Atlantic Ocean on the evening of September 3,

1939, felt a rumbling jolt. Some said it was like a cannon going off somewhere in the guts of the ship.

The intense impact of the explosion catapulted passengers into the air, causing immediate death when they landed on the deck. Some people were tossed over the ship's rails into the deep Atlantic. A young girl was killed by flying debris as she lounged in a deck chair. Crewmen working near the crippled engines were killed instantly. Kitchen workers were scalded by pots of hot liquids toppling from the massive stovetop burners. Stairs leading to the upper decks from cabins below were blown to shreds, leaving helpless passengers with no way out as rising waters filled their lungs.

Eleven-year-old Russell Park, traveling with his parents, was returning to America after a vacation in Ireland. Sitting with his dad in the library at the time of the explosion, Russell remembered hearing a loud bang. Then he was aware of his dad pulling him out from beneath a table that pinned him to the floor. People were screaming and yelling. He smelled something like hot metal or burning paint. He was scared but not seriously hurt.

Florence Kelly, 14, was on the *Athenia* with her mother. The two were traveling home to Ohio after spending the summer in Europe. When the explosion ripped through the liner, Florence was walking on the deck. She clung with all her strength to the railing, trying to steady herself. When the bone-jarring rocking of the ship finally stopped, Florence was left in total darkness. She knew her mother was in a nearby lounge. It seemed like forever before the two were reunited, just in time to find their way to a lifeboat.

Russell, Florence, and hundreds of other survivors made the treacherous descent into lifeboats—crafts that seemed sturdy enough when they were snugly attached to the solid passenger liner but that were now quickly filling with water. They were, however, the only means of survival. The survivors endured hours of cold, wet

Russell Park and his parents visited Ireland in the summer of 1939.
Library of Congress LC-USZ62-104598

Florence and Mary Kelly spent the summer of 1939 on the British Isle of Man. *Library of Congress LOT 13415, no. 701, LC-DIG-ppmsc-08688*

conditions, along with the constant fear that they might never make it ashore. Throughout the night they bobbed on the vast Atlantic Ocean, where, as one survivor put it, "every wave is your enemy."

What had caused the explosion? Some thought it was simply a mechanical problem. But everyone was thinking about the announcement of war between Great Britain and Germany just hours before. And some passengers said they had seen a submarine lurking on the surface of the water just before the explosion occurred. Florence thought it might have been an attack by an enemy plane, yet she hadn't noticed anything in the skies at the time. If there were enemy subs or planes in the area, were the lifeboats safe? Had the captain had time to send a radio call for help?

As the night wore on, distant lights pierced the horizon and ominous shapes loomed in the distance. The survivors, crammed in the lifeboats, worried about the advancing forms; were they friendly rescue vessels or enemy attackers?

If the approaching lights and shapes were friendly crafts, where would they take the survivors? Back to Europe, where war had broken out? Would the survivors be stranded, unable to go home to America until the war ended?

If the approaching shapes were enemy ships, what would the people on board do to the survivors? Fire upon the helpless lifeboats? Capture them and send them to prisoner-of-war camps?

What did the future hold for Russell and Florence? Would they ever again see their friends and families back home in America?

1

A KID'S WORLD

The kids of Cleveland, Ohio, were abuzz with excitement in May 1939: A new comic strip starring a hero called Superman began appearing in newspapers around the country for the first time. The comic featured someone everyone could look up to, and the Superman character was the creation of two young hometown fellows, Jerry Siegel and Joe Shuster. Stella Walsh, a 1936 Olympic track star and Cleveland resident, was doggedly training for the 100-meter and 200-meter races and the broad jump for the upcoming 1940 Olympics in Finland. People who had been at her house claimed Stella, a Polish immigrant, already had over 600 trophies and medals from world competitions stacked up in her bedroom. Zealous Cleveland Indians baseball fans looked forward to night games now that the municipal stadium was installing electric lights. And, best of all, school was soon to be out for summer.

Florence Kelly, a 14-year-old ninth grader at Maple Heights High School in a suburb of Cleveland, had more reason than most to look forward to the end of the school year. In June she and her mom, Mary, were traveling by ship across the Atlantic Ocean to the Isle of Man to visit relatives. Florence's dad, Harry Kelly, wasn't able to leave his job as manager of a chain of grocery stores, so his wife and daughter would set out on their own. Florence knew how lucky she was to spend the entire summer vacation in a faraway British island laced with sparkling

Florence Kelly and her mother, Mary. *Courtesy Florence Kelly Roseman*

beaches and ocean breezes. She knew many kids could only dream of a vacation like this because the Great Depression had caused many adults to lose their jobs.

About 400 miles from Florence, 11-year-old Russell Park was finishing up fifth grade in Philadelphia, Pennsylvania. Like Florence, Russell was an only child. Unlike Florence, Russell had been on family cruises before with his parents. Each year Alexander and Rebecca Park planned summer holidays to intriguing places. The summer before, the Parks had traveled on the *Queen Mary* to England, France, and Holland. Russell was fascinated with ships and sailing and looked forward to his annual trek to ports around the world. The Park family was anticipating a lovely summer visiting family in Ireland in 1939. They were ready to enjoy fine beaches, pleasant rail tours, and pristine seaside golf resorts.

In May as the Kelly and Park families planned their vacations, they weren't expecting any problems that would keep them from having fun-filled, relaxing holidays in Europe. The parents were busy packing and making travel arrangements. Florence and Russell were doing what kids did in 1939, having fun and sharing special times with friends.

Teenagers all over America were dancing to "Peckin' with the Penguins," "Dusting the Donkey (aka the Payoff)," and "Dipsy Doodle" performed by Tommy Dorsey, a popular band leader in 1939. He was one of Florence's favorites. She and her best friend, Eileen, loved big band music.

Most Saturdays the two girls hopped a city bus to downtown Cleveland, where they ate lunch and took in a movie. One of their favorite pastimes was attending spectacular events at the Palace Theater, where famous singers, dancers, and comedians performed. Florence and Eileen liked to go backstage after performances to ask for autographs from the stars.

Florence knew she would miss her dad and Eileen while on the Isle of Man. And how would she ever survive the summer without her beloved little gray striped cat, which snuggled under the covers with her at bedtime? But her dad had promised to take good care of her pet, and she knew Eileen would be eager to hear all about her lovely holiday when they were reunited in the fall.

In 1939 kids who loved reading and lived in large cities could go to public libraries to borrow books for free. In Philadelphia the name of the library was actually the Free Library of Philadelphia. Bookmobiles delivered books to kids in more remote areas. Those were welcome options for families who had limited money during the hard times of the Great Depression. But if parents could afford it, they could purchase children's books for one to two dollars at a bookstore.

There were plenty of good choices available for Russell in his quest for reading material about ships, travel, and history. Books about Rear Admiral Richard Byrd, an Arctic explorer and naval officer, and aviation pioneers Charles Lindbergh and Amelia Earhart were hits with kids Russell's age. Scouting magazines like *Boys' Life* or

American Boy taught kids how to make their own play-things like rafts, small boats, and kites. For dog lovers, a popular book was *The Three-Cornered Dog*, a story about the adventures of a boy and his three-legged dog in the Maine woods.

Philadelphia was a perfect place for a history-loving kid like Russell to live *any* time. It was one of the oldest cities in America, and it was chock-full of museums, historic buildings, and celebrated landmarks. Philadelphia was the birthplace of the US Navy, dating back to 1776. It became a major shipbuilding center, and in 1939 the Philadelphia Naval Shipyard still built and repaired the nation's ships. And, best of all, Russell's dad worked at the shipyard.

Fewer ships had been built at the Philadelphia ship-yard in the early and mid-1930s than in the past, but lately things had picked up. In April it had been announced that workers at the shipyard would build a craft that was the first of its kind in America. It was a 6,000-ton mine layer. The *Terror*, as it would be known, would be equipped to place high explosive mines in harbors and around naval fleets at sea, protecting them from enemy attacks in wartime.

The Philadelphia Naval Shipyard would charge the navy almost $10 million to build the *Terror*. And the 9,000 workers at the shipyard would be very busy with this craft and other new ships that the navy planned to build. It seemed Russell's dad would have plenty of work to do when he returned to his job after the family's summer vacation in Ireland.

Russell's dad worked at the Philadelphia Naval Shipyard, where ships like this were built. *Courtesy Library of Congress HAER PA, 51-PHILA, 709-9*

As Florence and Russell said good-bye to their classmates at the end of the school year and looked forward to the long, carefree summer that stretched ahead, the US government was thinking about letting 20,000 desperate refugee children move to the United States from Europe. Some citizens thought America must help these kids who were living in dangerous and life-threatening situations. Others believed the refugees would be a burden to Americans who were recovering from the Great Depression. "We must be hard-boiled and refuse to admit these refugees if we are to keep the benefits of America for Americans," a letter writer to a newspaper in California proclaimed. And a government official in New York said, "I don't think we can afford to let them in, because we have more needy people in this country than we can take care of."

And there were more unsettling events occurring in other parts of the world that worried America's leaders. As the Kelly and Park adults carefully laid out their travel agendas, news headlines were beginning to sound a little ominous. German dictator Adolf Hitler told the world his country was "one of the most heavily armed nations in the world." Italian leader Benito Mussolini said the Italian people were "not afraid of war." He added that his country had "many weapons and very strong hearts." Early in May, Hitler warned the world, "We may have to fight." Great Britain and France promised they would stand with Poland if Hitler's armies invaded, as many feared. And in the United States, government leaders set aside money for "the biggest defense program in American peacetime history" while hoping to stay out of the problems so far from home.

It all was enough to make the Kellys and Parks nervous about the world situation. But there were also many signs that calmed the two families. Every day newspapers reported the arrivals and departures of passenger ships between US and European ports. Tourists were regularly traveling back and forth across the Atlantic Ocean without any problems. Many people in Europe and the United States were hopeful that problems in Poland would be solved through talks between officials, not through war.

The US Congress had passed several Neutrality Acts, which meant if other countries went to war the United States would not take sides. It would stay out of the fights. President Franklin D. Roosevelt made a speech and said, "I have seen war on land and sea. I have seen blood running from the wounded. I hate war." There were many signs that life was going on as usual in the United States. The New York World's Fair opened in May and over 600,000 attended the first day.

If the Kellys and Parks had paid attention to only the scary news reports, they might have changed their travel plans. But the travel agent told Alexander Park that his family would be "perfectly safe" traveling across the Atlantic. The Kellys weren't terribly worried either. Harry Kelly was going to drive Florence and Mary to Montreal, Canada, where they would board the British ship *Athenia* for their trip to Europe. He also booked passage for their return trip at the end of summer.

A teenager who thrilled at the sight of famous film stars and a young boy who loved to read—two ordinary American kids who weren't thinking about the frightening actions of world leaders in May 1939. They happened to have some things in common. Both were confident kids who were comfortable spending time with adults and who looked forward to new ventures to unfamiliar places.

2

WORLD AT THE
BRINK OF WAR

Florence and Russell were lucky in many ways. Their dads had good jobs; their families had plenty of food and clothing; and they lived in America, where the government was stable. They felt safe and secure most of the time. They were even able to enjoy a few luxuries in life, such as European holidays.

However, many families in different parts of the world lived in fear in 1939. For 10 years the entire world had experienced very hard times. Governments and families were affected. Government leaders did not have money to keep parks, roads, schools, and hospitals in good condition. They couldn't pay back money they had borrowed from other countries. Factories closed. Businesses and banks failed. As many as 30 million people were out of work in the world.

Ten years was a long time to live with poor economic conditions. This time was called the Great Depression. People were getting frustrated. Many were ready for strong leaders to make things better. Another problem that led to a frightening world in 1939 was the fact that several major countries in the world were governed by dictators who had great power to wage war and to control their citizens' lives. The United States, Great Britain, and France were democracies, while dictators ruled Italy, Germany, the Soviet Union (now split into several countries, including Russia), and Japan.

In 1939 the rulers of Italy, Germany, Japan, and the Soviet Union had become popular by promising to greatly improve conditions for those who were suffering. For ordinary people who were desperate, these bold men and their ideas sounded good. And they offered simple explanations for the world's problems. They blamed certain groups of people.

Anyone who spoke against the leaders in control was in grave danger. In Japan Emperor Hirohito controlled the government along with a group of military men. In the Soviet Union Joseph Stalin and the Communist Party held power. Fascist leader Benito Mussolini was in control in Italy; and in Germany, Adolf Hitler led the Nazi Party.

In these countries the government controlled information in newspapers and on radio stations. Strict rules restricted many parts of daily life, work, and even art

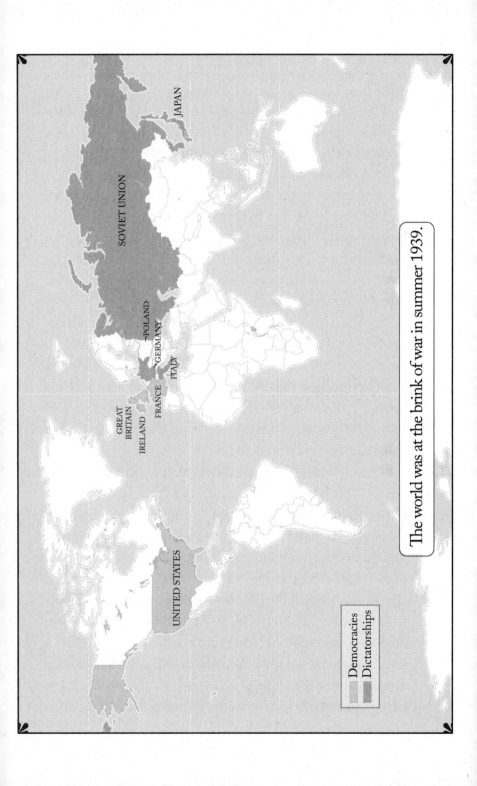

The world was at the brink of war in summer 1939.

Democracies
Dictatorships

and literature. Cruel police forces in these countries made sure people obeyed laws. Individuals had no rights. Ordinary citizens lived in constant fear of being viewed as disloyal, a crime punishable by torture or death.

"On every street corner spies were posted to listen to the words of the passers-by and make immediate arrests should they hear an utterance of discontent," an Austrian reported after Nazi Germany invaded and took control of his country in 1938. "We hardly dared to say a thing in our own homes."

In the Soviet Union Joseph Stalin purged, or removed, anyone who threatened his power. He used any excuse to explain his actions. In November 1938 a leader in the Communist Party angered Stalin. He was quickly removed from power. The reasons given: he was slow in killing people who were considered enemies. The man was arrested and executed.

Throughout the 1930s Germany, Italy, Japan, and the Soviet Union built up their military forces. This helped improve their economies, but it also gave their leaders more power. They wanted to be ready in case enemies attacked. They needed the military to help take over new lands. And a strong military was a sign of power. These countries increased the number of people in their armies, navies, and air forces. They built new warships, airplanes, and submarines. Factories turned out new military weapons like guns and tanks. Newspapers carried articles about the "mighty Soviet Power," Italy's "most powerful arms," and Germany's "invincible strength."

In Germany many people were forced into military service through the draft. Others joined by choice. They saw opportunities for careers in the army and navy.

Fritz-Julius Lemp was someone who wanted to join the German military. His dad had been an army officer, and Fritz wanted to serve his country too. In 1931, when he was 18 years old, he joined the navy, the Reichsmarine. He was noticed by his officers and was given

Fritz-Julius Lemp (most likely the man saluting on the left) was a German submarine captain. *Courtesy Naval History and Heritage Command, NH 111241*

opportunities. He went to submarine school and became a captain. By November 1938 Fritz was given command of a submarine called the *U-30*. Many Germans admired this patriotic navy man. But in September 1939 he forever changed the lives of hundreds of innocent people, including two American kids.

As the governments of Germany, Italy, Japan, and the Soviet Union increased their military might, they were eager to grow bigger by taking over other lands by force. They were bold and brutal as they swept into smaller, weaker regions. Many times they simply killed the people who lived there. Those who survived were forced to live under harsh new governments.

Japanese leaders wanted their country to be more powerful. They looked at China, a huge country in their part of the world. Invading China, they bombed cities and villages day and night from the air. When the army entered a region, the townspeople were robbed of their food and other possessions. Some were tortured until they turned over money they had hidden from their captors. They were forced to pay taxes to the Japanese. People were arrested for unknown reasons. In jail they were beaten with heavy sticks; some were beaten to death.

When food was in short supply, it was reported Chinese kids sat on street curbs waiting to catch leaves falling from trees. They gathered twigs and dug up small trees. They went after all parts of the plants to use for food. "Now small children hack away at the roots," a newspaper reported.

In April 1939 Benito Mussolini's Italian troops moved into Albania. The Albanian army was no match for the Italians. The tiny country was attacked by air and sea. Cities were left in complete ruin. Roads and bridges were blown up. Fields of crops were burned. Museums were "bombed, destroyed and ransacked" by the invading armies.

As these countries' armies moved to conquer weaker nations, people tried to escape before the invaders arrived. These refugees searched for safe regions in their own countries. Some were lucky enough to find refuge in other countries.

In China in 1939 it was not unusual to see large numbers of people wandering the roads with ragged bedding, cooking pots, and baskets of rice strapped to their backs as they fled the Japanese soldiers. Some had saved their precious animals, which plodded along with the families.

One man who had escaped the Germans in Austria found work in England as a butler. His dad had been a famous surgeon in his homeland, and he had been studying to become a doctor himself. Working as a butler was a very different way of life, but at least he was safe.

Another young Austrian refugee living in London in March 1939 recalled the horrors of life under the Nazis: "Our doorbell was rung. . . . When I opened the door, eight men stormed into our flat and without a word started their dreadful work of destruction. For three hours, three hours I shall never forget in my life, I heard

nothing but the sound of breaking glass and the crack-
ing of the fall of pieces of heavy furniture." The soldiers
broke up china, glassware, mirrors, electric bulbs, picture frames, flowerpots, and the birdcage. Everything—
chairs, beds, curtains, carpets, and clothes—was cut
into pieces.

The young man's father returned home as the Germans were destroying the apartment. He was immediately arrested. For a week there was no word of his fate.
"We did not know where he was nor what was going
to happen to him," the man said. Then one day his dad
returned home to the apartment littered with all their
shattered possessions. He described his father as "half-
killed" but grateful to be alive. Thousands of others
had been taken to prison camps, and others had been
murdered.

By August 1939 dictators around the world had made
great gains in expanding their lands by invading and
conquering vast regions of neighboring countries. Japan
had gobbled up chunks of China. Italy conquered Ethio-
pia and Albania. Germany took over Austria, Czechoslo-
vakia, and parts of Lithuania.

As these countries swept in to conquer more and
more territory, the major democracies of the world
used different ways to deal with the problem. Leaders
tried talking together, seeking to make agreements that
would be good for everyone involved. They punished
invading countries by refusing to trade with them. They
looked for ways to avoid war. Most adults remembered

very clearly the war that had engulfed the world roughly 20 years before. The Great War (later called World War I, 1914–1919) was still fresh in the memories of many. Millions had died. No one wanted to get involved in something like that again.

The world's democracies knew that something had to be done to stop these dictators from taking over the world. Germany's Adolf Hitler was especially frightening. He was telling the world that he was going to invade neighboring Poland. If that happened, what would nearby democratic nations do? Would they help Poland as they had promised? Would Hitler's next move be to invade France and Great Britain, countries that were friends of the United States? And how would that affect Americans?

Many Americans hoped they and their children were safe from all these problems happening thousands of miles away in other parts of the world. But as it turned out, decisions made by the world's leaders would have very real consequences for two American kids.

3

~~~

GREAT VALUE FOR YOUR TRAVEL DOLLAR

EUROPE ONLY A DREAM AWAY. TRANS-ATLANTIC SERVICE PLANNED. Newspapers across America flashed the almost unbelievable headlines. Pan American Airways was about to offer transatlantic travel in their "super flying boat."

The *Yankee Clipper* was scheduled to make its maiden flight in May 1939. The first trip across the ocean would carry 16 people from New York to Southampton, England, and would take 24 hours if all went well. None were paying customers because no one knew how safe the venture would be. Only a crew of seven and a few company employees would embark on this history-making air journey.

Pan American Airways promised "all the comforts of home" in its "all metal" flying boat that could reach speeds of 203 miles per hour and climb to 21,000 feet. With a wing span of 152 feet and length of 109 feet, the machine sported propellers 14 feet in diameter.

The interior of the *Yankee Clipper* was something of unimaginable wonder. The upper deck housed the flight crew. The passenger quarters were located on the main deck and consisted of five cabins, each holding 10 people

The *Yankee Clipper* was not available to the general public in the summer of 1939. *Courtesy Library of Congress LC-H22-D-6000*

during the day and 6 at night. There was a dining room, dressing rooms, a bathroom, and a galley for food preparation. Deep cushioned sofas and small tables were sprinkled throughout the main lounge. Smokers were free to roam throughout the skyliner at will.

After the airplane had made five round-trip flights successfully, Pan American Airways would offer the service to paying customers. It could carry 74 passengers. The company made the outlandish prediction that sometime in the future they would have a plane capable of transporting as many as 300 passengers across the ocean. And they claimed their flights would be as regular as rail transportation was currently. It was a time of wonderment for travelers who were accustomed to taking passenger ships between America and Europe, a journey that typically took about two weeks.

Flying across the Atlantic Ocean to Europe was only a sensational newspaper story for Florence and Russell as they looked forward to their summer vacations in 1939. Although Florence had traveled to Europe when she was a baby, she was too young to remember the trip. So this seemed like her first transatlantic sea voyage as well as her first visit to the Isle of Man. Russell's family vacation to Europe in the summer of 1938 had prepared him for the family's next adventure.

The Park family's 1938 voyage had been especially exciting because they had traveled to and from Europe on the "grandest ocean liner in the world." The *Queen Mary*, "alive with beauty, energy and strength," was the choice of Hollywood stars, European royalty, and world leaders as they went back and forth across the Atlantic Ocean. The luxurious floating paradise boasted the best in style and comfort. Its lounges, swimming pools, ballroom, sports courts, and five dining rooms offered the best in grand travel for the rich and famous.

Boarding the *Queen Mary* in New York City, the Parks had arrived in Southampton, England, on June 27, 1938, and had spent time seeing the sights of Europe. They reboarded the luxurious liner at Cherbourg, France, for their return trip and arrived in New York later in the summer.

It had been an unforgettable vacation for Russell, and in the summer of 1939, he was eager for his next sea voyage and European holiday. However, he would not be traveling on the *Queen Mary* this year. The Parks would sail on the *Transylvania* on their way to Ireland, and Alexander had purchased tickets on the *California* for their return trip. But that was just fine with Russell. He would have two different floating treasure chests to explore.

The Park family planned to leave on Tuesday, August 8, from the port of New York. No one knew it at the time, but it would be one of the final voyages the *Transylvania* would make carrying vacationing passengers. Soon the mighty ship would be in the service of the British military transporting fighting men to war.

As Alexander, Rebecca, and Russell Park made plans for their summer holiday, Harry Kelly was busy lining

The Park family sailed on the *Transylvania* on their way to Ireland. *University of Glasgow Archives & Special Collections, Papers of James Adamson and William Robertson, GB248 DC101/0617*

up boat tickets for Mary and Florence to leave from Montreal, Canada, on the British passenger liner the *Athenia*. It had been a harsh winter, and some Canadian harbors were still frozen over in April and May in 1939. The *N.B. McLean*, a Canadian Coast Guard ship called "one of the world's most powerful icebreakers," had spent the spring crashing through the thick ice along the St. Lawrence River to clear the harbors for the approach of passenger liners. Two other icebreakers, *Lady Grey* and the *Saurel*, had cleared the area around Montreal.

Florence and her mother had tickets on the *Athenia* for their trip to the Isle of Man. *Author's collection. Gjenvick-Gjønvik Archives*

The Kellys didn't expect ice problems in the harbor in early June when they were scheduled to board the *Athenia* in Montreal. First there would be an almost 600-mile drive from their home in Ohio to Montreal, but Harry wanted his wife and daughter to enjoy a worry-free trip that didn't include changing luggage between home and the Isle of Man. The easiest route for them started in Canada and arrived in Liverpool, England. The return tickets were also on the *Athenia*, and they were set for September. Florence and Mary would have three glorious months visiting family on the Isle of Man. Harry was sure the *Athenia* would provide a safe, carefree voyage for mother and daughter.

The Park family was confident about their ship too. The *Transylvania* had been built by the Fairfield Shipbuilding and Engineering Company, a well-known and highly respected shipbuilder in Glasgow, Scotland. The ship weighed nearly 17,000 tons and was powered by steam. With a length of over 500 feet and breadth of 70 feet, it was a massive craft. The ship's "excellent lines," "most up-to-date" navigation instruments, and engine room "of the latest design" offered an "imposing appearance."

The *Transylvania* made its maiden voyage in September 1925 traveling between Glasgow and New York City. Throughout the 1930s the ship carried tourists between Europe and the United States and during summers to Bermuda and the West Indies. It also carried US mail to Europe. By 1938 the ship was ready for some updates.

In May the ship was back home in Glasgow being fitted with new "solid propellers" to increase its 16-knot cruising speed to 17 knots. Cabins were being redone and made larger. Hot and cold running water and new clothes closets were added to all the cabins. The *Transylvania* would be more luxurious than ever before. In June 1938 the ship was back on the seas providing transatlantic crossings again.

When the Park family traveled from their home on Market Street in Philadelphia to New York City in August 1939, their destination was Pier 45 at the foot of West 10th Street, where they boarded the *Transylvania* to Europe. They passed through a new terminal, a modern "fireproof building of brick, masonry, and steel." One entire wing, complete with elevators and baggage conveyors, was "streamlined" to speed up travel "in every way" for passengers waiting to board transatlantic liners.

It was a warm, cloudy day when Russell and his parents climbed the gangplank to the *Transylvania* for their journey. Their first-class tickets meant they had access to every comfort imaginable on their floating hotel. The main lounge featured a decorative fireplace, carved ceilings, and stately white columns. It was furnished with soft chairs and a grand piano. The cabins were decorated with fancy wallpaper and curtains. The beds were made of dark, rich woods, and the floors were covered with lush fringed carpets. Plump, fluffy comforters topped the beds. Silk chairs completed the sitting area in the cabins. Glass-top tables held vases of fresh flowers.

The dining rooms held long tables that sat ten, covered with crisp white tablecloths and napkins. Passengers were served a variety of courses by head waiter George Owsley and his staff. Tall arched mirrors soared to the ceiling. Ornate plaster carvings adorned the walls.

Chef Jack Drysdale offered *Transylvania* passengers orange juice and herring for breakfast. Lunch and dinner included meats, broccoli, asparagus, coffee, and tea.

For dessert passengers could chose French pastries or ice cream. Chef Drysdale had spent time on ships that traveled to India, and he was especially skilled at preparing Indian food. He was also known for his beef steaks and vegetables soaked in wine.

After eating the rich, high-calorie meals, passengers sometimes made their way to the ship's gym, where the equipment promised to "exercise every muscle in the body." Here fitness instructor Jack Denovan Jr. helped them stay active over the course of the trip. Passengers could gallop on electric rocking horses, tangle with a leather punching bag, or learn jujitsu from instructor Denovan.

Any passengers who spent time with the captain of the *Transylvania* learned that the man had always loved the sea and ships. Captain David Bone was born in Glasgow, Scotland, and had spent as much time as possible on the docks when he was a boy. "After school I liked to get as near the ships as I could," he said when asked about his childhood. "And I read everything about the sea I could beg or borrow."

Captain Bone was "broad of beam" and "very strong." But what made him so special was that he was also a writer and illustrator of books. His love of reading led him to install a "floating bookshop" on the *Transylvania*. A ship library at his disposal and a sea captain who wrote books—it was more than a book-crazy, sea-loving boy like Russell could hope for. In the popular slang of the day, this was sure to be a swell, keen, snazzy trip to Ireland.

When Florence and her mother set out on their summer vacation, they traveled on another beautiful ocean liner. *Elegant, cozy, charming.* Those were words used to describe the *Athenia*. The travel brochures claimed the ship offered "famous cuisine, personal service and entertainment" all representing an "outstanding value in ocean travel" and "a great value for your travel dollar."

Like the *Transylvania*, the *Athenia* was built at the Fairfield Shipbuilding and Engineering Company in Glasgow, Scotland, where over 7,000 workers worked at building 15 ships at once. Its maiden voyage had taken place in 1923. Departing Glasgow, the *Athenia* had stopped at Belfast, Ireland, and Liverpool, England, to pick up passengers going to Quebec City and Montreal, Canada. It was a route that the liner routinely made for years.

The shipbuilder's brochure promised that the 13,500-ton ship blended "novelty and a sense of adventure" in its design. The 540-foot-long liner was the "last word in modern ship construction," according to the brochure. And most important of all, the ship was safe and secure, with watertight bulkheads and doors throughout and two large masts that held radio antennas for constant contact with land.

In addition to having the best safety features, a newspaper advertisement claimed, the *Athenia* would provide vacationers with "all the comforts of a first-class hotel" and a voyage filled with "pleasure and contentment."

Three levels of cabins were offered for round-trip tickets: cabin at $264, tourist at $236, or third class at $182.

As Florence and her mother stepped onto the *Athenia* in Montreal on June 4, 1939, they were greeted by the all-Scottish, seasoned crew of more than 200. The captain was James Cook, who had made 15 trips between the United States and Europe in his first year as commander of the liner. He had first gone to sea at the age of 16 and had served with the British navy during the Great War. Captain Cook's chief officer was Barnet Mackenzie Copland, a Scot who had gone to sea at the age of 15 and had served on the *Athenia* longer than the captain. He was an able-bodied seaman who had earned the respect of the captain.

Florence and Mary were led to their tourist-class cabin, which contained a small sink with hot and cold running water and a porthole that allowed an ocean view. A steam radiator provided warmth when the sea air made for chilly nights. Florence took the upper bunk, giving her mother the lower. The two appreciated the "quiet elegance" of the ship.

Mother and daughter took their meals in one of the dining rooms, where white-jacketed waiters stood at attention with crisp linen towels draped over their arms. Domed ceilings supported by marble columns soared overhead. Their meals, offered in several courses, were typical British fare consisting of roast beef, chicken, peas, carrots, mashed potatoes, and custard.

Florence and her mother shared a cabin on the *Athenia.* *Author's collection. Gjenvick-Gjønvik Archives*

Multiple stately yet comfortable lounges, smoking rooms, and drawing rooms were scattered throughout the ship. Rich leather chairs and sofas, plants, and art created an inviting feeling in the lounges. Dark wooden beams graced the ceilings, and there was a room filled with desks for writing letters.

The nursery was complete with a fireplace, stuffed teddy bears, dolls, a rocking horse, and a life-sized teepee. Painted scenes covered the walls. There was a library stocked with newspapers, books, and magazines. The hospital was staffed with a doctor and nurse. And passengers could have a haircut or manicure at the hairdresser's and barber's shops.

Florence and a 16-year-old girl named Jean from Ottawa, Canada, struck up a friendship on the journey to Europe. They took part in the many activities offered: shuffleboard games, tennis, concerts, or movies in the evenings. Sometimes they strolled on the deck or rented deck chairs and enjoyed the gentle sea breezes.

As they walked they passed dozens of lifeboats stacked along the edges of the decks. There were enough to hold all the passengers and crew. They had been in drills and knew the rules for using the lifeboats in case of an emergency.

Fortunately the seas were calm, the lifeboats remained in place, and Florence and her mother enjoyed a quiet voyage over the entire 3,000 miles of ocean. After days on the sea the *Athenia* safely docked at Liverpool, England,

and mother and daughter embarked on their summer venture.

Later in the summer, Russell and his parents arrived at Glasgow, Scotland, where the *Transylvania* docked on August 16. From there the Park family traveled to Ireland, where they joined their relatives.

Soon these two American kids would cross paths as world events forced Russell and Florence to share a frantic escape and a slice of history.

4

FRANTIC ESCAPE

Wild lions roaming the streets of London. Prowling tigers wandering through English villages. Menacing chimpanzees pouncing at unsuspecting kids in Liverpool. It was a scenario no one wanted to imagine. But it was a very real possibility.

Lions, tigers, and chimpanzees were safely housed in zoos across the United Kingdom. In August 1939 as war seemed close at hand, zookeepers pondered how to protect humans and animals should the enemy attack. The public was reminded that skittish lions and tigers would likely hide from humans; however, chimps were immensely powerful creatures and in their terror could be dangerous.

Zoo staff prepared for the worst. If there was time, the animals would be moved to facilities outside major cities. In case of a surprise attack, zoo personnel were trained in first aid. But if the enemy caused extreme damage to enclosures, zookeepers were prepared to use rifles to kill the magnificent beasts who had become their friends.

Zookeepers and others had good reasons for making plans for an enemy attack by air or sea. It looked more and more likely that Germany and Great Britain would go to war. The German leader, Adolf Hitler, had been acting very aggressively toward other countries for more than a year. He had threatened to invade Poland. Leaders in Great Britain said if Hitler invaded neighboring Poland, Great Britain would see it as an act of war. France and Great Britain told the world they would come to Poland's aid if German armies moved in. People around the world hoped Hitler would back off.

Despite the scary news coming out of Europe, Americans continued to travel there. Some, like Florence and Mary, had planned far ahead and decided to follow through with their vacation in spite of unsettling reports of danger.

After leaving the *Athenia*, Florence and Mary boarded a small boat for the four-hour journey from Liverpool to the Isle of Man. Around them, the citizens of Liverpool were well aware of the threatening situation in Europe, but they tried to carry on with their normal lives, determined to set fear aside.

Liverpool was a bustling seaside port with hundreds of warehouses and factories surrounding the docks. The citizens were hardworking people who made their livings as miners, dockworkers, truck drivers, and railroad hands. Some worked in the shops that lined the city streets. There were meat markets, bakeries, and cinemas where kids watched American stars like Judy Garland, Mickey Rooney, and Ronald Reagan in the latest movies from Hollywood. High school and college students swam, danced, bowled, and joined regatta races and golf tournaments. In many ways, it was a typical British city. Although they didn't know it at the time, the summer of 1939 would be the last peaceful one for a very long time.

Mary Kelly was certainly thinking about the problems in the world and was more than a little worried. But Florence was "in vacation mode" and could only think about the exciting summer that stretched ahead. Many aunts, uncles, and cousins awaited her arrival on the Isle of Man, and she couldn't wait to see them. It was a thrilling time for her.

After entering port at Glasgow, Scotland, Russell and his parents left the *Transylvania* and traveled to their destination in Londonderry, Ireland, about 275 miles northwest of the Isle of Man, where the Kellys were visiting.

The ancient walled city of Londonderry (also known as Derry) was a treasure-filled place for a curious boy who was enchanted with people and places from the past. A summer navigating the nooks and crannies of a city with a history that began in the year 546 was a dream come true for Russell. Tales of Irish chieftains, marauding invaders, warfare, and bloodshed were just the type of intriguing mysteries from the past that could capture the imagination of this adventuresome boy from America. Ageless relics, yellowed documents, and priceless artifacts like rusty padlocks and keys from the city gates were housed in the museums, galleries, and churches of the old city. Londonderry promised days of climbing on battered old cannons, walking along the 18-inch-thick city walls, and marveling at the mighty fortresses.

The Parks could stroll the city streets where tailors, drapers, vintners, and goldsmiths had practiced their crafts in the past. Or the family might play a round of golf on one of the two courses available to visitors. Taking a break from sightseeing, they could enjoy icy glasses of a new drink just introduced to Ireland—Coca-Cola. And when they tired of the man-made sights, the Parks could climb the rolling hills that surrounded the city. From that point they shared a panoramic view of the River Foyle and the outlet to the sea.

Meanwhile, Florence and her mother spent the summer absorbing the irresistible charms of their island paradise. The Isle of Man was home to the Kellys' extended family, and it was a center for tourism where vacationers toured ancient stone houses and carefully preserved castles.

Florence delighted in getting to know her cousins, who introduced their American cousin to their day-to-day lives. She split her time between the cities of Ramsey and Laxey. Some days Florence joined the kids at school, where the students prodded her for details about her American way of life. Other times she strolled the lovely beaches or visited nearby farms. From a hilltop she watched the world-famous Tourist Trophy motorcycle races held each summer, when the roads across the island were closed so racers from all over the world could zoom through a 30-mile loop at speeds up to 130 miles per hour.

Over the summer Florence made frequent jaunts to other parts of the United Kingdom. She visited Scotland, Wales, and Ireland; toured Stonehenge and Loch Lomond; and marveled at the sights in London. "It was a fabulous summer," Florence remarked.

As Florence and Russell enjoyed their summer vacations, scary things were taking shape all across the United Kingdom. For some time refugees had been fleeing their homes in eastern Europe and making their way to the United Kingdom and other lands that they hoped would welcome them and provide safety from invading armies. Many nations did welcome refugees. "The fate of refugees is not a matter to which we can show indifference," one newspaper warned. But there were limits to the generosity shown by the countries that agreed to take in refugees. Many drastically limited the numbers of refugees permitted within their borders, partly because of the high cost of helping. And most warned against illegal immigration, which was called "one of the most terrible of human problems."

In addition to helping refugees, public officials in the United Kingdom faced other difficult decisions with the threat of war looming. By mid-August, preparations for war were underway. Galleries and museums were moving their treasures to secret hideaways; banks took important files, machines, and safes to offices outside major cities; hospitals were blast-proofing operating rooms.

By the end of the month ordinary citizens were directly affected. Plans were made to close cinemas and other amusements in major cities to avoid large crowds that might attract enemy bombs. Police departments recalled officers who were on holiday, and future leaves were canceled. Additional nurses, first aid workers, and ambulance drivers were being trained.

Gas masks went on sale for 2 shillings, 6 pence; steel and concrete bomb shelters were being constructed; merchants at London's open-air markets reported fewer people purchasing pets because the animals would probably have to be put down in the event of war. However, for those who chose to keep their pets, it was recommended that kennels be built that were blast-, gas-, and splinter-proof.

Blackout drills were held in large cities, citizens were urged to limit phone calls because of heavy demand by the government and military, and there was a possibility that sporting matches would be canceled if war was declared.

Across the country plans were made to move children, expectant mothers, and elderly people away from large cities in the event of war. Officials thought rural areas would be safer from enemy bombs. Teachers were called in to their schools on Saturday, August 26, for training to help move students to the countryside. Housewives were told to prepare for emergency food shortages. The Animal Welfare Society met to discuss how to deal with the 40,000 horses, 18,000 pigs, 6,000 cattle, 400,000 dogs, and 1.5 million cats that they estimated resided in London.

Back in the United States newspaper articles and radio news reports relayed the bad situation in Europe. Americans were urged to leave Europe as soon as possible. In mid-August Florence's dad called from Ohio. He knew Florence and Mary had tickets to return to America on September 2 on the *Athenia*. "You'd better try to get home earlier," Harry begged. Mary tried but could not get an earlier ticket on any passenger liner headed to the United States or Canada.

"The situation has reached a point which makes it advisable for American travellers to leave England," read a statement from Joseph Kennedy, American ambassador to the United Kingdom. "All those who do not have any important reason for remaining are urged to return to the United States without delay." Americans took the ambassador's urgings seriously.

Russell and his parents were scheduled to return to Pennsylvania in late August. They already had tickets on the British liner the *California*. But in mid-August the shipping company contacted Alexander Park to tell him that he would need to find another way home for his family. The *California* had been taken over by the British navy and would be made into a warship. Alexander did not want his family stranded in Europe, possibly for the duration of the war. Thousands of American and Canadian tourists, as well as desperate refugees, were trying to get out of Europe. Alexander frantically searched for spots on another passenger ship.

Shipping ticket offices were swamped, jammed with people trying to buy tickets to North America. "There are thousands ready to pay a fortune for your berth," a travel agent told an undecided ticket buyer. "Do you want it or not?" he asked. The buyer quickly made a decision to snatch up the ticket before it was too late.

Finally Alexander found three tickets for his family on the *Athenia*. It was headed to Canada instead of the United States, but Alexander believed he was incredibly lucky to have snatched up the last chance to get out of the frightening situation in Europe. He felt sure he'd found his family a certain path to safety.

The *Athenia* was scheduled to leave Glasgow, Scotland, on Friday, September 1, heading to Belfast, Ireland; to Liverpool, England; and then across the Atlantic Ocean to Montreal, Canada. It would pick up fleeing passengers at each of the stops. The Parks would join the liner at Belfast and the Kellys at Liverpool.

On the morning of Friday, September 1, at 4:45 AM, Germany invaded Poland just as Hitler had warned. The world waited to see what Great Britain would do.

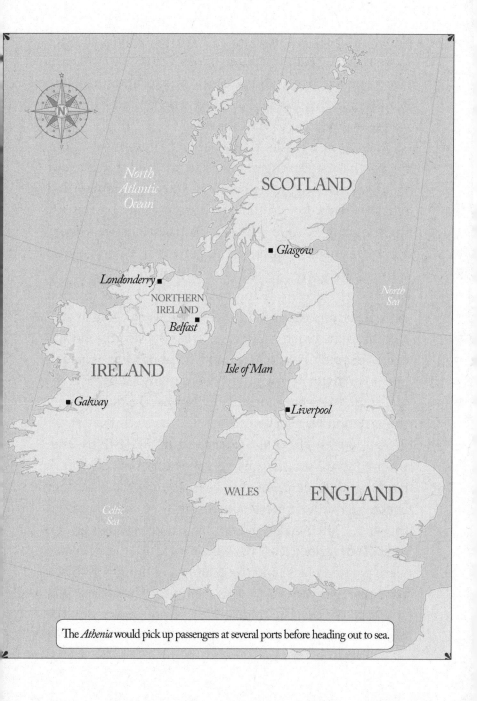

The *Athenia* would pick up passengers at several ports before heading out to sea.

People who were scheduled to leave on the *Athenia* were extremely nervous. Captain James Cook was worried. Everyone had been talking about war for months. Now it all seemed very real. However, the United Kingdom was still at peace—at least for now.

The *Athenia* made its way out of Glasgow at about noon. The 420 passengers who had boarded talked about the overcrowding in the hotels as desperate tourists and refugees had come to the city hoping to get on the last ships leaving Europe. Lines at train stations were long, and it was nearly impossible to get a taxi. Underground train stations were closed, sandbags were in place, and bomb shelters were being built rapidly. People carried gas masks, and thousands of children were being evacuated from the city to safer rural areas. Radio announcers urged people to keep calm and go about life as usual. However, in any crowd there were many "drawn faces" and "pinched expressions" showing that the public knew the situation was very serious.

At 8:00 PM the *Athenia* arrived at Belfast, Ireland, where 136 passengers and refugees boarded. The Park family got on there. As soon as Russell spotted the liner in the harbor he noticed something very peculiar about the ship. "The *Athenia* did not have a light showing," he said. He described it as "dark as a tomb." All the windows were painted black, and the doors were hung with black curtains. Everyone knew this meant the ship's crew was trying to conceal the huge craft from the enemy on the open seas.

Nine hours later, on Saturday, September 2, the ship stopped at Liverpool to add 546 more passengers, including Florence and Mary. Onboard it became obvious to everyone that this would not be a typical cruise. Hundreds of extra passengers had been taken on. Every square inch of the liner, including the gym, was fitted

Passengers spent time relaxing on deck chairs on the *Athenia* **when the weather was pleasant.** *Courtesy Library of Congress LC-DIG-fsa-8d37009*

with sleeping cots. Even the swimming pool was covered and lined with beds.

Florence and her mother were happy to have a cabin to themselves. Russell's family was split up. Alexander was assigned to a cabin with another male passenger. Russell and his mother shared a room with other women.

As the liner embarked on its transatlantic voyage, it carried 1,102 passengers and 316 crew. That was 200 extra passengers and 41 extra crew. Despite the crowded conditions, most passengers did not complain. They felt extremely lucky to be on a comfortable ocean liner headed for the safety of North America. They were leaving danger behind. Someone reminded the passengers, "Others would give their lives to be on board the *Athenia*."

Both Florence and Russell were going home with memories of pleasant summers. Each had shared warm get-togethers with loving relatives, toured exciting cities, and seen some of the United Kingdom's most historic sights. Russell, with fond memories of Ireland, looked forward to another sea voyage, spending days exploring the *Athenia*. Florence couldn't wait to return to school back home in Cleveland, where she would tell friends about her wonderful vacation on the Isle of Man.

The two had no way of knowing that the world they were leaving behind would never be the same after that summer. Some of the cities they had visited would be

A German submarine lurked in the waters of the Atlantic Ocean.
Courtesy Library of Congress LC-DIG-ppmsca-23122

severely damaged by enemy bombs over the next five years. Some of the family members they were leaving would not survive the war. And for those who did survive, life would be forever changed. Death and destruction would blanket the lands the two American kids had cherished so much during that last summer before war.

Florence and Russell had no idea their frantic escape from land would lead to terror at sea—and that memories from their short time on the *Athenia* would stay with them for the rest of their long lives.

5

ATTACK AT SEA

A s the *Athenia* moved west into the Atlantic Ocean on the evening of September 2, the passengers were relieved to have escaped the uncertainty of Europe. They were wondering what actions Great Britain would take against Germany as a result of the invasion of Poland. But they felt relatively safe.

The crew had blackened the portholes, the doors were covered in black cloth, and no one was allowed to use flashlights or matches outside after dark. And Captain Cook had decided to take a slightly different route, hoping to avoid any enemy ships that might be expecting them along their usual course.

However, all the precautions taken to slip undetected through the waters of the wide Atlantic would prove to be useless. And the passengers were sadly mistaken in their sense of security. No one on the *Athenia* knew it, but a threatening German submarine lurked in the waters directly in their path, waiting for the moment to strike. The *Athenia*'s voyage began calmly, but that would soon change.

Florence and her mother were glad to be on the open sea heading back to the safety of their home in Ohio. Florence was concerned for the relatives and friends she had left behind in the United Kingdom, but she was glad to be bringing her memories of the summer home with her. She had taken scads of photos with her new camera, a gift from her dad before she had left home. And she had packed other souvenirs in her luggage, including a beautiful kilt she had bought in Scotland. As Florence recalled, "We never thought anything could happen to us."

As soon as passengers arrived on the ship, they were required to take part in lifeboat drills. It was always part of the routine on a big liner like the *Athenia*. Russell had been through it many times before on his travels, so when he and his parents arrived on the *Athenia*, the drill was old news to him. But his parents seemed a little worried about it. Passengers were assigned to specific lifeboats based on where their cabins were located. Because Alexander was in a separate cabin from Rebecca and Russell, he was assigned to a different lifeboat. As it turned out, that would be a life-changing detail in the days ahead.

The *Athenia* was equipped with 26 lifeboats. *Courtesy Library of Congress LC-DIG-fsa-8d37008*

As Florence, Russell, and the other passengers settled in for their long journey across the Atlantic, Oberleutnant Fritz-Julius Lemp waited. The commander of the German submarine *U-30* was watching for enemy ships carrying troops and war materials such as guns and ammunition.

On the morning of Sunday, September 3, Florence and Russell attended church services in the ship chapel with their families. They thought a quiet, peaceful Sunday afternoon stretched before them. But about 11:00 AM word began to spread throughout the ship. Great Britain had declared war on Germany. Captain Cook had received a radio message reporting the unsettling news. The ship's crew posted announcements of the British prime minister's message to the people of the world throughout the liner.

"This morning the British Ambassador . . . handed the German government a final note stating that, unless we heard from them by 11 o'clock that they were prepared at once to withdraw their troops from Poland, a state of war would exist between us. I have to tell you now that no such undertaking has been received, and that consequently this country is at war with Germany," British Prime Minister Neville Chamberlain said.

Now passengers and crew who had felt safe began to show signs of fear. With war declared, everyone knew that German submarines would attack enemy ships. And the *Athenia* might be a target. However, the rules of war stated that passenger liners were off-limits in wartime. Would Germany obey the rules? No one knew with certainty. But Adolf Hitler and his armies had shown no mercy for anyone or anything that stood in their way in the past.

Captain Cook didn't want to show any uneasiness to the passengers. Still, he instructed the crew to prepare the lifeboats. They required passengers to once again take part in a drill. Passengers were reminded to bring a small case filled with warm clothes and to grab a lifebelt.

By afternoon everyone had calmed down a bit. Fresh, gentle breezes swept over the decks, a perfect day for relaxing. While Florence relished a day of reading and strolling the deck, Russell had more adventurous plans. The curious boy set out on an expedition to conquer the interior of the massive ship that would be home for several days. He explored everywhere passengers were permitted and a "few places where they were not allowed." When he spied a jumble of spare anchors in a pile tucked into a nook on the deck, he couldn't resist a daring climb up the iron mountain. By the end of the day no one would have described him as "the cleanest boy in the world," Russell recalled years later.

Russell and his dad went to the dining room at 5:30 for dinner. Rebecca was feeling seasick so stayed in her cabin. After the evening meal of baked salmon served on silver platters, Russell and his dad decided to visit the library, where Russell picked a book about trains from the children's shelves. He settled in at a glass-topped table. The pair didn't know it at the time, but Russell's love of reading, which led them to the ship's library, would prove to be a lifesaver. Before the night was over, the library would turn out to be one of the safer places on the ship.

Florence and her mother had eaten an early dinner also. Afterward Mary went to a lounge to read, and Florence strolled on the promenade deck. It was a peaceful, relaxing time for the mother and daughter, but these would be the last tranquil moments they would experience for quite some time.

While the *Athenia* passengers were finishing up their meals, Oberleutnant Lemp and his crew of 43 sat above the surface of the Atlantic watching for enemy ships. Just around sundown, they spotted one, about 250 miles west of Ireland, approaching on the far horizon. No one knows exactly what he was thinking, but it was at this moment that Lemp made his fateful decision to attack. The *Athenia* was his target. The time was 7:40 PM.

Did Lemp consider that the ship might carry young kids like Florence and Russell? Would it have made a difference if he had realized there was a woman lying in one of the ship's hospital beds, unconscious and unable to escape a sinking ship? It would be years before the world learned just what this German officer probably knew and thought as he made a decision that would forever haunt the unsuspecting passengers on the *Athenia*.

Lemp ordered his crew to submerge *U-30* and to prepare to release two torpedoes into the advancing ship. The crew obeyed their commander and launched the torpedoes. One hit its mark, blasting a gaping hole in the port side of the *Athenia* at the waterline. The second missed. Then the Germans fired two more torpedoes toward the *Athenia*. The first missed the passenger liner, and the second stuck in the submarine, causing fear among the crew. They again tried to eject the torpedo, and this time it successfully left its tube. However, it did not hit the *Athenia*.

Lemp ordered the crew to return to the surface. By now a bright moon allowed the Germans to witness what they had done. In the distance the *Athenia* was slowly sinking. The *U-30*'s radio operator George Hoegell heard the *Athenia*'s distress calls on his radio. And the German crew was close enough to see the panic on the ship as a result of the attack. Oberleutnant Lemp ordered his crew to leave the area as quickly as possible.

The torpedo had struck the *Athenia* in the boiler and engine areas in the greatest depths of the ship, where the main electrical generators were located, causing the electricity to fail. The men who were working there were killed instantly or severely injured with burns covering their bodies. A huge oil tank was damaged, spewing oil in the interior of the ship and through holes into the surrounding ocean. Men preparing meals in the kitchen were scalded by hot pots of food that toppled from the stoves. Passengers who were in their cabins below deck were thrown violently from their beds. Some were drowned as water gushed into the rooms. Others who were able to get out to the hallways were overcome by rising waters that carried floating bodies. Stairways that should have given them an escape route to the upper decks had been severely damaged or blasted away, preventing people from climbing to safety.

Witnesses said it felt as if the ship gave a "shiver" and sounded "like a giant fire cracker being put in a huge tin container." Ceilings in the cabins and dining rooms had collapsed, and splintered boards littered the floors.

Shards of glass and mirrors speckled the decks. Smoke filled the passageways. Bitter fumes hung in the air. There was darkness all around.

Above deck, Florence felt and heard a "terrific explosion" that caused the ship to "rock from side to side" and forced her to clutch the railing to avoid falling overboard. She saw two people who had been sitting on a hatch jettison into the air. Florence watched in horror as their lifeless bodies hit the deck next to her.

Her thoughts turned to her mother. It seemed an eternity before Mary emerged from the nearby lounge to find her daughter. She had been thrown to the floor as she read, but she was happy to be alive and only a little bruised. Their passports and her purse containing all their money were somewhere in the shambles of the lounge, but it was too dark to look for them. And there wasn't time. "We were told to go immediately to our lifeboat stations," Florence said.

When the torpedo struck, Russell and his dad were in the library. As an adult Russell remembered a "loud metallic bang" that propelled him from his chair as he read his train book. It was only a short time before Alexander, searching in the dark, found his son under a crumpled tangle of furniture. Shattered glass was all around. Russell remembered being "very scared" as he repeated over and over, "Something's happened."

In those first few moments no one knew what had happened. "My first thought was that we'd been bombed by an airplane," Florence said. "But there was no airplane." Many of the passengers, who had been hearing and witnessing the Germans' threats for months, believed the *Athenia* had been the target of the Germans.

Terrified children crying for parents, husbands screaming their wives' names, mothers grasping their sobbing babies—everyone wanted desperately to be with their families. A variety of sounds could be heard as refugee families cried out for their loved ones in their native languages.

But there was confusion as people tried to escape the lower sections of the ship or make their way from a severely damaged dining room where there was "absolute carnage," a survivor later said. Crew members carried unconscious, bleeding victims in their arms. Some passengers who had been on deck at the time of the explosion were tossed over the railings into the sea. Their "frightful screams" were heartbreaking to those who watched and survived to tell their stories. Some were saved; others disappeared into the swirling, dark waters.

Smoke was thick in the air. A survivor remembered a "heavy powdery smell" greeting stunned passengers. Throats were "parched" and "filled with a kind of fine soot," she recalled. A "funny odor like gas" spread throughout the cabins that had been so badly damaged. She remembered "an ugly cloud of brown powder" hanging "like an evil eye" over the water. "I could smell burning paint, hot metal," Russell recalled.

Bodies were everywhere, floating among splintered metal and wood in the flooded hallways belowdecks and charred and lifeless on lounge chairs where they'd been relaxing on deck only minutes before. It was impossible to avoid them. Russell stumbled over "a burned bundle of rags." Passengers running to their lifeboat stations simply stepped over them. Another survivor said someone stopped to cover the face of a dead man "staring vacantly into space" on a deck chair.

"I stumbled over one man, who was obviously dying," one survivor recalled. "His eyes were rolling around in a way I had never seen in my life."

Maisie Levine was in the dining room at the moment of impact. Her one-year-old baby, Stephen, was asleep in their cabin. "I went up one deck to my cabin," Maisie said. "Everything was dark. I went in and got my baby and wrapped a blanket around him." Maisie made her way to her lifeboat station and handed her precious bundle to a stewardess who carried little Stephen into the lifeboat. Maisie followed.

The lifeboat drills the passengers had been through had not been a waste of time. As the ship's whistles blasted six short signals followed by one long bell—the warning to abandon ship—the passengers who were able to move hastened to their assigned lifeboat stations. Some tried to return to their cabins to get their lifebelts. Others grabbed lifebelts they found scattered about the deck.

Alexander steered Russell to his station, hoping to see Rebecca there. When she didn't appear, Alexander told his son he was going to her cabin. He directed Russell to get into a lifeboat as soon as the crew allowed loading.

Many passengers were in a dining room when the explosion took place. *Author's collection. Gjenvick-Gjønvik Archives*

Then Alexander disappeared below into the darkness of the ship's interior. Russell was alone.

Florence and Mary had found their way to their lifeboat station. As they approached they were told the boat had room for only one more. They looked at each other and shook their heads. They would stay together. Let someone else take their place in the boat.

It turned out to be a lucky decision. As the lifeboat was lowered into the swirling ocean alongside the sinking *Athenia*, the ropes that held the boat broke. All the people in the lifeboat were dumped into the sea. Miraculously, all survived but were thoroughly soaked and covered in oil that had leaked from the *Athenia*'s damaged engines.

Florence and Mary made it into the next lifeboat lowered to the sea. When they touched the surface of the water, Florence flung her hand over the side of the boat. It suddenly hit her, "Oh, my gosh, we are right down on the Atlantic Ocean." It had seemed so far away, and less threatening, as she viewed it from the height of the *Athenia*. It also occurred to Florence that she had never learned to swim.

Russell continued to wait for Alexander and Rebecca next to the lifeboat station. When the crew started to load the boat his mother and he were assigned to, she and Alexander still had not appeared. His dad had told him to get on the boat, but Russell decided to wait. Each time another lifeboat filled and was dropped into the sea, he held back. Finally, he heard a crew member shout, "This is the last one."

Russell turned one last time to search the deck for his parents. They were nowhere in sight. He climbed onto the lifeboat as the crew lowered it to the murky waters of the Atlantic Ocean. Finally, the ropes lowering the lifeboat to the ocean were cut, and it dropped to the sea. *We were on our own!* Russell recalled later.

His last thoughts as the lifeboat pushed away from the sinking *Athenia* were of his beloved parents. He pictured his dad and mom as he had last seen them. He thought about his dad going to the cabin for his mom. "It took a lot of courage for him to do this," Russell said many years later.

By 10:00 PM on September 3, the last living person had left the *Athenia*—at least that's what everyone believed. Before launching the final lifeboats, the crew had counted dead bodies on the ship and come up with the number 50. Captain Cook reminded them about Rose Griffin, a woman who was lying unconscious in the ship's hospital from a fall she had suffered the first day on the ship. During the rush to load lifeboats, there had been confusion about Rose. The crew thought she was safely installed on a lifeboat.

Time for every living person to leave. No one was certain how much longer the *Athenia* could stay afloat. The captain knew the ship would soon be at the bottom of the deep, dark sea. At about 11:00 PM he issued his final command as captain of the magnificent *Athenia*: "Abandon ship!"

6

NIGHT OF TERROR

"All of us are sick now and the sounds of gagging and vomit are all that can be heard," a young woman who survived wrote in a news article she titled "Worst 36 Hours I Have Lived Through." The passengers who had been lucky enough to survive the explosion on the *Athenia* were crammed into the 26 lifeboats that had been launched from the decks of the liner. But they soon realized danger was still very much all around. And although they were no longer on a large vessel that was slowly sinking to the bottom of the ocean, they were adrift on small, water-filled boats crowded with sick and injured people.

Others had not survived the transfer from the ship to the lifeboats. It had been a dangerous, risky ordeal.

The heavy wooden boats were lowered from the decks of the *Athenia* into the swirling ocean waters with ropes. Some broke, dumping people into the water. Or the two ropes—one at each end of the boat—didn't always lower at the same speed, causing the craft to tip to its bow or stern. Some people fell into the water trying to jump from the *Athenia* to the lifeboats.

Getting into the boats was not an easy undertaking because the lifeboats swung out from the decks of the ship. Sometimes passengers had to leap several feet. Some boats bumped against the sides of the sinking *Athenia*, causing passengers to tumble about as they were lowered to the sea. In some cases, the lifeboats had been lowered to the sea first and people slid down ropes to get to them. Their hands were badly burned by the friction. One boat was almost lowered on top of another that had not gotten out of the way soon enough.

The transfer to lifeboats was especially difficult for the injured, the elderly, small children, and parents with babies. And many of the passengers had been suffering from sea sickness when the *Athenia* was hit, so they were already feeling weak. When they safely reached the lifeboats and realized they were at the mercy of the Atlantic Ocean, they could only hang their heads over the sides of the boats and vomit. Many were not able to move to the sides and were sick on the floor.

As the lifeboats moved away from the sinking liner, they were chased by the sounds of screams coming from the direction of the *Athenia* as passengers jumped from

This mother wrapped her little girls in men's clothes to shield them from the cold. *British Pathé*

the ship or as lifeboats capsized. "Never shall I forget those screams," one survivor later remarked.

"I saw one man gasp for breath and die," a woman said about a victim who spilled from a capsized lifeboat. "It was horrible."

Others were distressed by the "ominous form" of an overturned lifeboat in their path, causing "a silent shudder" to pass through the survivors as they floated past the doomed craft. Would they soon meet a similar fate?

As they settled into the lifeboats, many survivors were startled to see several inches of water in the bottoms of the boats. And even more terrifying was the fact that the water was quickly rising. Each boat was designed with holes in the bottom so that when they were stored on deck and rain water collected in the bottoms, the crew could pop out the plugs to drain the water. Now that the boats were filled with humans and were bobbing around the ocean, many of those plugs were missing. Seawater was seeping in.

Some of the boats had *Athenia* crew members among the passengers, and they knew more about sea travel and survival than most. On Florence and Mary's boat a crew member advised moving quickly away from the sinking liner. He knew that as it descended to the ocean floor, it would suck any objects on the surface down with it. And that included wooden lifeboats overflowing with men, women, and children. "Row, row as fast as you can!" the crewman shouted.

But first the heavy wooden oars had to be lifted onto the oar locks that held them in place on each side of the boat. Florence helped a woman and the crewman as they struggled to secure the oars. Finally, they were in place, and everyone who could help moved the hefty oars in unison. They were so heavy that as many as three people handled each oar. Slowly, they steered the boat away from the sinking *Athenia* and out into the "vast nothingness of waves and darkness."

Russell found himself in a boat with mostly women and one crew member, who also urged everyone to locate an oar and help row away from the *Athenia*. The crewman, an "aged waiter from one of the dining rooms," wasn't a professional sailor, but he directed the

Survivors helped row in the crowded lifeboats. ©*Imperial War Museums (HU 51008)*

work. "Row one, row two," he ordered. When a group rowing in the front of the boat dropped an oar, Russell jumped to retrieve it from the water. The rowers headed the boat into the wind.

Throughout the night the boats drifted on the water. At times the waves were ten feet high, sloshing over the sides. The moon was bright, but clouds sometimes covered it, leaving the survivors in total darkness as they quietly bobbed on the water. A light rain fell. In some of the lifeboats, soft sobs could be heard over the night air from the passengers who were separated from family members. Some didn't know if their families had escaped the sinking *Athenia*, but others had witnessed their loved ones in their final moments of life. A mother who had watched helplessly as her baby fell into the sea moaned distraughtly. In other boats it was so quiet that babies slept soundly in their mothers' arms.

In Florence's boat everyone seemed to be peaceful. "Nobody was panicky or screaming," Florence said. Someone began to sing a well-known hymn, and many joined in. At other times, people could be heard praying. At one point during the long night, Florence turned to her mother and asked if she thought anyone would come to their aid. "Oh yes, they will find us. They will find us," Mary assured her daughter.

Russell was cold and wet from the splashing oars and from water seeping up to his waist. People used their shoes to bail water. Someone asked the crewman what had happened on the *Athenia*. Someone suggested that the boiler had blown up. The crewman said he didn't know.

The surface of the ocean was littered with debris: abandoned life rings, furniture from the liner, broken beverage bottles. Dark pools of oil hugged the surface. Most disturbing was the occasional body floating among the wreckage. One survivor said there was "something unearthly about the whole scene."

Red lights dotted the waters as people lit flares hoping to attract the attention of friendly ships. But many survivors feared the flares would make them targets for the enemy. No one knew with certainty that the *Athenia* had been attacked by the Germans, but it was a rumor that many passengers believed. And if it was true, were the Germans still lurking in the darkness?

Some people were so sick and cold that they didn't mind if they met up with the Germans. Hands were raw with blisters after hours of rowing. Everyone was exhausted. Some had not eaten anything since noon on the day of the attack. In boats that were very crowded, passengers who were near the oars had to crouch to give rowers room to swing the oars. The big waves lifted boats high into the air, slamming them back down to the surface of the water.

"I didn't care whether we were picked up by a German ship or any other," one survivor said. "I was so sick. And I was wet and cold."

While many shivered from the drenching seawater, others were coated in thick, black oil. The explosion had caused oil from the *Athenia* engines to spill into the surrounding sea. The lifeboats were floating in the slick, slimy mess. Survivors who were pulled from the water were covered in oil. And the waves that splashed into the open lifeboats were oily too. People in the boats soon became coated with black muck.

Very few were dressed for a cold, wet night on the open sea. Many who had been in bed when the explosion occurred were in their pajamas or robes. Because it was late summer, people wore only lightweight clothing. Passengers who were dining at the time of the tragedy were dressed in elegant dresses and dinner jackets. Women wore silk stockings and high-heeled shoes. Florence wore the type of clothing any girl her age would have worn at the time—a cotton dress with white socks. Most had not been able to return to their cabins to gather extra clothing. Throughout the early hours in the lifeboats, people shared. Those lucky enough to have coats wrapped them around shivering children and babies. People were wrapped in curtains they had grabbed from the cabins.

Some of the survivors were suffering from injuries they had sustained during the explosion or as they transferred from the liner to the lifeboats. There were bruises, fractured bones, rope burns, and sprained ankles. Blood oozed from open cuts. Some injured people had slipped into unconsciousness and lay in the bottom of boats. Everyone was suffering from exposure to the cold and from exhaustion. Ten-year-old Canadian Margaret Hayworth, who was traveling with her mother and sister, had been seriously injured when a piece of debris from the explosion delivered a deep gash to her forehead. She slipped in and out of consciousness.

A stewardess held little one-year-old Stephen Levine in a boat that quickly filled with water. As his mother, Maisie, rowed throughout the night, the baby never closed his eyes to sleep. "He wasn't sleeping because he knew there was something wrong. His eyes were wide open all the time," Maisie recalled.

Some of the lifeboats were overcrowded. Others were not filled to capacity. Russell's boat was approached by one of the few motorized boats that the crew were using. The officers were bringing people from overcrowded boats to boats that weren't full. They asked if Russell's boat could take on more people. "No!" came the clear reply from the jam-packed vessel. But they said they could use some additional crew members who could help row. The officer promised to return with some able-bodied men who could help. But no one ever came.

Although all the lifeboats had quickly moved away from the *Athenia*, the passengers could see lights on the wreck in the distance. The crew had started generators soon after the attack, and they supplied power for the lights. Some people were spooked by the "eerie hulk" of the sinking passenger liner. Others felt comforted. "It was encouraging to see the lights on the *Athenia*," Russell said. "While she was afloat, we still had hope."

After what seemed like "an eternity" but was actually about eight hours, the people in the lifeboats thought they saw lights on the horizon. These were not lights on the sinking *Athenia*. Someone said they looked like "far-off Christmas trees." As they peered into the distance, the lights grew closer. And some people believed they could make out the outlines of ships.

"Soon we could see an outline," a survivor recalled. "It was a man-of-war. A German perhaps! It seemed bearing right down upon us. Was it going to ram us?"

When Florence's boat lifted on the swell of a wave, she and her mother saw the lights in the distance but feared the survivors in their lifeboats were too small to be seen across the wide expanse of ocean. Russell and his fellow passengers spotted lights too. And before long it was obvious that a vessel was slowly closing in on them. Then it stopped. Russell became aware of shapes moving about in the waters surrounding them.

"This ship kept coming towards us and finally it came so close there was absolutely nothing we could do to get away from it," a terrified survivor said.

Both hope and fear gripped the hearts of the survivors of the *Athenia* as they drifted on the waters of the Atlantic in those early morning hours of Monday, September 4, 1939. Most were unaware that Captain Cook had sent a distress signal before he and his last crew members abandoned ship. No one knew that Oberleutnant Lemp, the German commander who had attacked the *Athenia*, had heard Captain Cook's call for help.

Were the approaching lights friendly seamen or enemy German sailors? One thing was certain. If they were Hitler's navy coming to finish the job started by Oberleutnant Lemp's *U-30* submarine crew, there was very little chance the *Athenia* survivors, who floated helplessly on the wide-open stretches of the Atlantic Ocean in their small wooden crafts, would survive a second attack.

7

INCREDIBLE RESCUE

"We were aware of large dark shapes moving about us. A destroyer closed in on us slowly. . . . It got close enough for us to make out the detail. We were close enough to recognize men on deck," Russell later wrote.

The rowers in Russell's lifeboat frantically tried to move the boat toward the lights that were creeping toward them. But it was very difficult to wrestle the waves, and they soon found themselves adrift. The approaching lights were moving very slowly. It seemed they would never arrive. And Russell's lifeboat couldn't make any headway. They continued to drift in the darkness.

As time passed, a wind shift began to move Russell's boat toward the lights. It was clearly a craft headed their way. But in the darkness Russell could make out other large dark shapes on the water too.

Russell's boat continued to move toward the lights, but it was rough going. Finally, as dawn broke, the murky shapes and mysterious movements became clear. The shapes were large ships that were picking up the survivors of the *Athenia* as they floated on the Atlantic in their wooden lifeboats! It would be several hours before the people in Russell's lifeboat were picked up, but when their turn came, Russell was one of the first off the boat.

The ships had responded to Captain Cook's SOS call from the sinking *Athenia*. It had taken them hours to reach the site of the attack. The *Knute Nelson* was the first to arrive in the area where the lifeboats bounced in the waters of the Atlantic. The Norwegian freighter had begun to pick up survivors about 2:00 AM. Soon after, a Swedish yacht, the *Southern Cross*, arrived on the scene. By about 4:30 AM two British destroyers, the *Escort* and the *Electra*, came to help. Around 7:00 AM a British destroyer named *Fame* had joined the effort to provide antisubmarine patrol. And *City of Flint*, an American freighter that was in the area, also came to the rescue of the *Athenia* survivors.

Because the lifeboats were scattered over a wide swath of the ocean, some survivors spotted the distant lights on the horizon earlier than others. The first sightings occurred a little after midnight, but, of course, the passengers in the lifeboats were not aware that the lights came from friendly ships. And because the waves became very choppy during the night, some—like Florence—could catch only a quick glimpse of the lights when they were at the top of a wave. "We realized they were headed toward us," Florence said.

The *Knute Nelson* slowly worked its way toward the lifeboats. It was about two hours before some of the people in lifeboats could see clearly the name on the side of the rescue ship—realizing it was not a German ship.

At last, the horrible ordeal was about to end. Families who had been separated hoped to be reunited. Warmth, dry clothes, and hot food couldn't be far away. And, most of all, the fear of another attack was set aside as the people in the small lifeboats saw the sturdy rescue ships, including powerful British warships. But it was far too soon to rejoice. There were hours of terror, tragedy, and heartache ahead for the survivors of the *Athenia* disaster.

For those injured, sick, cold, and exhausted survivors it was no simple task to steer their boats through the choppy, churning waters to the rescue ships. It required immense strength that many no longer had. To some it seemed an impossible task.

"It's no use!" a rower cried.

"Come on, come on, we're almost there," another passenger urged.

"Come on, let's go!" a fellow rower shouted.

Finally, when the lifeboats had made their way alongside the rescue ships, the survivors looked up. The decks seemed like the highest mountains on earth. They were in fact 20 to 30 feet up from the lifeboats. And the waters were rougher than ever.

The crews of the rescue ships tossed rope ladders over the sides of the ships for survivors to climb. Holding one end of a rope, they flung the other end down to the waiting lifeboats. The survivors were instructed to tie the rope around their waists so they could be hauled up. None of these feats were easy for the weary passengers. And what about babies and small children?

Some were tossed into the air and crew members on the rescue ships caught them. In other cases sailors slid down on ropes to the lifeboats, grabbed hold of the babies' clothes with their teeth, and with the precious bundles dangling from their mouths, carried them up the rope.

Stephen Levine was not quite a year old, too heavy for his mom, Maisie, to hold while climbing a rope ladder as it bounced against the hull of the *Escort*. "They raised my baby to the destroyer in a pail. He stood up in the pail and held the rope while he was pulled up. He cried going up. That was the only time he cried," Maisie proudly explained.

As Florence's lifeboat made its way toward the *Escort*, the weary passengers cheered. The British sailors worked together to bring passengers to the deck. Two sailors leaned over the destroyer's deck holding a rope ladder. Two more sailors held tightly to the feet of the first two to make sure they didn't fall overboard.

People in the lifeboat grabbed the ladders and got
their feet up. As quickly as possible, the sailors grabbed
the passengers under the arms and pulled them up to
the destroyer's deck. No one wanted to see a passenger
fall between the lifeboat and the warship, which was a
real concern. It would have meant certain death.

Survivors were wrapped in blankets. ©*Imperial War Museums (HU
51010)*

Everyone in Florence's boat made it safely onto the *Escort*. "Oh, it was wonderful. They were so good to us," Florence said. "They were so pleased that they had rescued us."

Florence and Russell both happened to be picked up by the *Escort*; however, they didn't meet at the time. Russell's boat had waited for quite some time as others unloaded. Finally, as his boat drifted among the other empty lifeboats, Russell's turn came a few hours after daybreak. He was transferred up the ladder "into many helping hands."

Other passengers were not as lucky as Florence and Russell. Some lifeboats overturned as they tried to ease alongside the rescue ships. "Frenzied screams" could be heard across the waves as boats capsized, spilling people into the rough waters. The swells carried victims away from the ships. Some people slipped below the surface, never to return. The crashing waves drowned out their calls for help. A woman cried out for her child, but her screams were drowned as a wave closed over her. A baby dressed in a "brief night shirt" shot to the surface and was grabbed by a man, who pulled it to safety. A young girl fell between her lifeboat and the rescue ship she was trying to board. She never was seen again.

A mother watched in horror as her son toppled into the water from an overturned boat.

"Geoffrey! Geoffrey!" she screamed.

"Here I am, Mom," a voice came across the waves. The lucky boy was pulled to safety, and the two were happily reunited.

As several lifeboats clustered around the *Knute Nelson* a horrendous disaster occurred. One of the boats floated toward the stern of the freighter, where the large propellers sat. Suddenly the captain, unaware of the smaller boat's location, started the engine, and the propellers began to turn, churning the water. The propeller blades sliced through the lifeboat, instantly killing some of the passengers. Others were thrust into the swirling waters. Some were saved.

Not long after this, another mishap occurred. This time it involved the *Southern Cross*. As several lifeboats gathered around the Swedish yacht waiting to be rescued, the waves thrust one under the stern of the *Southern Cross*. About 50 men, women, and children were tossed into the sea. The crew of the yacht quickly climbed into empty lifeboats and tried to pick up the people who were scattered around the surface. Many were saved, but others drowned.

One very lucky boy was picked up by the Swedish sailors from the *Southern Cross* after being on four different lifeboats throughout the night. His first encounter occurred when the boat he was on capsized as it was being lowered from the *Athenia*. The boy survived the fall and swam to another nearby boat, which he occupied for most of the night. When the rescue ships arrived, the boy's lifeboat headed toward the *Knute Nelson* but capsized before reaching it. He was forced to swim to another lifeboat. When the *Southern* Cross appeared on the scene, the boy's lifeboat made way for it. But that lifeboat also met with disaster, and the boy was thrown out. Once again, he swam to another lifeboat—his fourth—and was rescued at last by the *Southern Cross*.

The crew of the *Escort* quickly made changes to take in the survivors. They prepared food for the hungry

Survivors arrived on shore wrapped in blankets after being rescued. *Courtesy of the National Library of Ireland*

guests. Florence had plenty of hot tea, biscuits, soup, and crackers. The crew hastily set up blankets and canvases as hammocks and beds for the weary survivors.

Florence and her mother slept soundly for the first time in hours. Russell was led to a hammock, where he slept for only about an hour. About 10:30 AM he was wakened by someone who said, "She's going down. Do you want to see her?"

It was the *Athenia*. The huge passenger liner was still visible to the survivors on the *Escort*, and some wanted to watch as she sank to the ocean floor. But Russell was too tired. He wanted to sleep. Others watched as the liner's bow heaved up out of the water. Then, slowly, the massive liner that had promised its passengers a voyage filled with pleasure and contentment and all the comforts of a first-class hotel began to sink out of sight. And then, "suddenly all that was left of her disappeared," a survivor recalled.

Luckily, not long before the *Athenia* sank, one of the officers on the *Electra* asked his crew about Rose Griffin, the woman who had been in the ship's hospital when the explosion occurred. It was discovered that she had not been rescued from the sinking liner. The decision was made to send some crew members back to the ship to get Rose.

It could be a dangerous undertaking; the officer knew that the liner could go down at any time. Boarding lifeboats once again, the crew rowed back to the *Athenia* and found it in a precarious position but still on the surface.

They climbed aboard and made their way to the hospital, where they found an unconscious Rose in a bed. They carefully loaded her onto the lifeboat and made their way back to the *Electra*.

Later that day on the *Escort*, Russell awakened from his deep sleep and realized he was hungry. Going in search of food he came upon some of the crew, and they provided him with his first meal (a meat sandwich, marmalade, and hot tea) since he and his dad had shared their last meal in the *Athenia*'s dining room. Then he set out to explore and to look for his parents. He hoped they had been rescued and were on the ship with him. But no one knew about Alexander and Rebecca.

As he explored the *Escort*, Russell saw a "large white yacht" not far away. He later learned it was the *Southern Cross*. He watched as passengers transferred from the yacht to the *Escort*. He learned that the yacht needed to transfer some of its passengers because it was dangerously overcrowded. Later he was told some of the passengers from the *Southern Cross* had been moved to the American freighter, *City of Flint*, which would take survivors to Canada. *Southern Cross* passengers were given the choice to transfer to *City of Flint* or one of the rescue vessels going back to Europe. Russell didn't know it, but his mother was on the *Southern Cross* and was one of those people transferred to the *City of Flint*.

Florence and her mother spent most of their time sleeping after being rescued by the *Escort*. One of the British sailors had seen how cold Florence was in her wet, thin dress and gave her a pair of his bell-bottom trousers. She wore them under her dress to keep her legs warm in the cool Atlantic breezes. They would end up being a treasured object that she kept all her life as a reminder of the kindness shown by her rescuers.

City of Flint took some survivors to Canada. *John F. Rogers Collection Nova Scotia Archives accession no. 2004-047 no. 50*

After all the lifeboats had been emptied and all the survivors were safely settled on the rescue ships, the ships began to leave. *Southern Cross* resumed its voyage to the Bahamas after transferring all its *Athenia* survivors to the *City of Flint* or the *Escort*. *City of Flint* headed to Canada. The two British warships, *Escort* and *Electra*, set out for Greenock, Scotland. The *Knute Nelson* made its way to Galway, Ireland.

All the survivors were happy to be out of the lifeboats, but danger and uncertainty were still present. The survivors on *City of Flint* were content to know they were going in the direction of their original destinations, Canada and the United States. But the survivors on the other rescue ships, *Knute Nelson*, *Escort*, and *Electra*, were going back to Europe and war.

Florence and Mary wanted to go home to Ohio, where Harry anxiously waited; Russell wanted to get back to Pennsylvania, where he hoped to be reunited with his parents.

Florence and Russell both wondered when they would see America again. Would they be spending the war in Europe, where German armies threatened terror and bloodshed? Their experience on the *Athenia* had made it clear that the Germans showed little mercy for their enemies. The thought of being trapped in Europe terrified these two American kids.

8

~~~

THE WAIT

"We were afraid Hitler was going to use chemical warfare. We all had gas masks," Florence remarked years later, as she talked about returning to Europe after being rescued from her night of terror on the open sea. Florence joined millions of frightened Europeans who were prepared for the worst now that Germany and Great Britain were at war.

And although Florence had expected to be on her way back home to Ohio and far from the terrifying events taking place in Europe by Tuesday, September 5, she found herself once again entering the United Kingdom. Everywhere she looked, there were chilling signs of war preparation.

Both British destroyers, *Electra* and *Escort*, docked at Greenock, Scotland, early in the morning of September 5. The *Electra* carried 238 *Athenia* survivors; the *Escort*, 402. Slowly the weak, tired passengers made their way down the gangplanks. Ambulances waited in the yards as injured survivors were brought to them. Several were taken to local hospitals. Rose Griffin, the woman for whom the *Athenia* crew had returned just before the

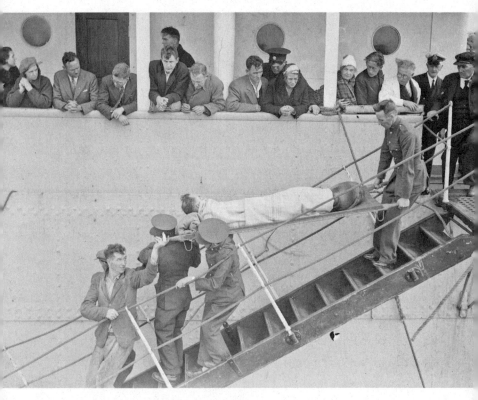

Some survivors had to be taken off the rescue ships on stretchers.
Courtesy of the National Library of Ireland

liner sank, was still unconscious and was carried on a stretcher to a hospital. Sadly, she would not survive. She died September 17 at the Royal Infirmary in Greenock.

Word had spread around town that some of the *Athenia* survivors were coming to Greenock. There was a crowd at the docks waiting to greet them. As they walked off the ships dressed in their unusual costumes, it might have been a comical sight to anyone who hadn't heard their story of survival at sea. They had been through a terrible ordeal. And they had spent the last 24 hours on military destroyers. Although they had been well cared for by the sailors of the *Electra* and *Escort*, many of the survivors were in shock and distress. They had not been able to bathe or comb their hair. Those who had been covered in oil had not been able to remove all the residue from their hair and skin. They were dressed in the clothes they had been wearing when the explosion occurred. Some wore their pajamas, nightgowns, or bathrobes and were wrapped in blankets. Others covered themselves in curtains they had taken from the *Athenia* as they rushed to the lifeboats. Some had been given military uniforms from the sailors. Many were barefoot. Some still wore their elegant evening clothes.

Because the authorities were unsure of many details related to the disaster, they were eager to interview the survivors. And no one was certain about the number of passengers who had been killed on the *Athenia* or had drowned before being rescued. It wasn't known with certainty that the sinking had been caused by a German

Injured survivors were taken to hospitals in the United Kingdom.
Courtesy of the National Library of Ireland

torpedo. There were many questions. The people who
had been at the scene of the disaster could solve some
mysteries, the authorities hoped.

Government and emergency officials set up stations
to talk to the passengers. They wanted answers, and they
wanted to help the survivors. They hoped to connect

family members who had been separated. They knew the survivors had only the clothes on their backs. Many had nowhere to stay and no money for hotels, transportation, or food. There were children, like Russell, who had no family members with them. What would happen to them?

As word spread quickly throughout Greenock, more people began to arrive at the docks. They weren't just curious to see the survivors of what many believed to be an enemy attack. They also wanted to help. People brought coats, pants, shirts, skirts, socks, and shoes to give to the survivors. They also brought food. Store and restaurant owners donated to the cause.

Plans were quickly made. Most survivors would be taken by bus to hotels in Glasgow, Scotland, only 25 miles from Greenock. There, people could relax until something could be done to get them to their homes again. Many of the survivors were Americans and Canadians. How would they cross the Atlantic safely? Would they be stranded in the United Kingdom until the war was over? No one knew how long that would be. There were many problems to solve. But for now, the survivors were happy to be dry and warm.

Florence and Mary had no money, and they had lost their passports. They were among the survivors taken by bus to Glasgow, where they were dropped off at the Beresford Hotel.

When Russell arrived in Greenock, he ran into the man who had shared a cabin with his dad on the *Athenia*.

The Beresford Hotel was a welcome home for survivors.
Glasgow City Archives D-CA 8/2962

He offered to take care of Russell until the authorities could find a family to take him in. The two boarded a bus for Glasgow, where they were set up in one of Scotland's finest hotels.

Russell was glad to see the man who had shared his dad's room. The man, whose name Russell never knew, had some very interesting news to share. Only a short time before the last passengers had left the sinking *Athenia*, the man had run into Alexander Park. He was making his way to the *Athenia*'s stern. Russell, who knew the ship well, knew his dad was heading directly toward the most badly damaged area of the liner.

It was the first news he had heard about either of his parents since being separated from them. Russell felt hopeful. But he was anxious too. He now knew his dad had stayed on the sinking ship until the last moment. But he had last been seen going into a very dangerous section of the ship. Did he make it out on one of the lifeboats?

As Florence, Russell, and the other passengers rescued by the *Electra* and *Escort* settled into their hotels in Glasgow, the 430 people who had been rescued by the *Knute Nelson* were taken to Galway, Ireland. The mayor and his wife had pulled together a welcoming committee of medical workers, bus drivers, and hotel owners. Even the Girl Guides (similar to the Girl Scouts) volunteered to help make the survivors feel welcome and safe. Just as the Scottish people had opened their homes, businesses, and hearts to the passengers of the *Electra* and *Escort*, the Irish people showed great kindness to their *Athenia* guests. Many of the *Knute Nelson* passengers were taken to private homes, hotels, or schools to wait for news about their next steps.

Florence and Mary were anxious to be reunited with Harry Kelly. But they knew that was not going to happen as quickly as they had planned when they set out for home on September 2. They were eager to get word to Harry, to let him know they were safely back in Europe. They wondered what he had heard about the *Athenia*. They knew newspapers and radios had spread word about the disaster all over the world. Harry wouldn't know whether his wife and daughter had survived.

It had been a terrifying few days for Harry back in Ohio. Just before falling asleep on Sunday night, September 3, he had listened to the news on the radio. There was plenty of talk about war in Europe, but he knew his family was on their way home on the *Athenia*. He was glad they had been lucky to get on one of the last passenger liners leaving behind the scary events in Europe.

About midnight, Harry was awakened by the jangle of the phone. It was a friend. "When are Mary and Florence coming home?" the friend asked.

"They're on their way," Harry replied.

"What ship are they on?" the friend inquired.

"The *Athenia*," Harry said.

"The *Athenia* has just been sunk!" the friend exclaimed.

There was no chance of Harry returning to sleep that night. It was the beginning of endless hours of phone calls to government officials as he frantically tried to learn the fate of Mary and Florence. It would be three days of agony before he knew if his beloved wife and daughter were dead or alive.

Meanwhile, Mary and Florence had moved to the Buchanan Arms Inn in the village of Drymen, where they were staying at the expense of a Scottish family named Henderson. They wanted desperately to call Harry, but communication lines were slow and unpredictable during those first days of war. They would have to be patient.

As they waited, the people of Scotland showed their generosity. Although she had no money, Florence was taken to a department store, where she was given a new set of clothes: underwear, shoes, skirt, two blouses, and a brown coat. She cherished the bell-bottom trousers the sailor had given her, but they weren't considered suitable attire for a young teen in 1939. She needed another dress. She had only the one she was wearing when she boarded the *Athenia*.

William and Millicent Henderson "adopted" some of the survivors at the Buchanan Arms Inn. They said they wanted their guests to go away with pleasant memories of their stay in Scotland. So every day the family came to the inn and took Mary and Florence on tours around the area.

The stay at the inn was meant to be temporary. Mary and Florence had been interviewed by government officials and said they wanted to return to the Isle of Man, where their relatives would be happy to welcome them. But they were told there were no boats going to the island. They said they also had family in Liverpool, England. So it was decided that's where they would go until they could find a way back to Ohio.

Just before leaving the Buchanan Arms Inn, Mary and Florence finally managed to get a phone call in to Harry in Ohio. "I was in tears. I was so excited to hear his voice," Florence recalled.

Russell also stayed in a hotel for a few days. He and his dad's cabinmate went to a meeting to hear a government official from the United States talk to the survivors. Russell was told the official was named Kennedy. It didn't mean much at the time, but as an adult Russell long thought it was Joseph Kennedy, the American ambassador to the United Kingdom. Later, Russell learned that the official was actually the ambassador's son John F. Kennedy, the future president of the United States!

Shortly after this meeting, a family invited Russell to stay with them until he could return to the United States. The man who had shared a cabin with Alexander Park and had cared for Russell at the hotel turned him over to the Cameron family.

Just before Russell left the hotel to go with the Camerons he received a telegram. It was from his mom's cousin. The telegram contained some very exciting news for Russell. His mom was alive! He learned she had been rescued by the *Southern Cross* and transferred to the *City of Flint* during the rescue operation. In fact, Russell had been very close to her when he watched the transfer from the deck of the *Escort*. This was fabulous news, but

Russell wondered about his dad. There was no mention of Alexander in the telegram. What did that mean? Did anyone know where Alexander was?

All the while the survivors were being cared for by the Scots and the Irish, American government leaders were making plans to send a ship to the United Kingdom to bring the survivors home. But it took time to arrange. And it would take more than a week for the ship to make the voyage from America to the United Kingdom.

Meantime, Florence and Russell passed the time waiting. Over 200 miles separated the two. But Florence in Liverpool and Russell in Glasgow both saw what war meant for ordinary people in the United Kingdom. Russell remembered the time as "a terrifying experience." There were daily air raid drills in which people practiced moving quickly to bomb shelters. At night streets and buildings were dark; lights were not allowed because they made it easy for the enemy to attack by air. Gas and food were rationed since they were needed for the military. Ordinary citizens would have to get by with less.

Both Florence and Russell got gas masks, which would provide protection from poisonous gas if the enemy dropped deadly chemicals from planes overhead. Florence carried hers in a little box slung over her shoulder with a strap. It was another souvenir she would keep all her life.

Store owners made the most of the situation. They put up signs that promised, SHOP IN SAFETY, SHELTER AVAILABLE FOR ALL CUSTOMERS. They advertised special wartime merchandise: SLACKS FOR SPEEDY DRESSING IN AN AIR RAID and GAS-PROOF FOOD CONTAINERS. And for the kids: WHEELED TOYS FOR EVACUATED CHILDREN and GAMES TO LIGHTEN BLACK-OUT EVENINGS. Store owners offered fashion tips: FOR BLACK-OUT NIGHTS, WEAR WHITE. And restaurants changed the menus to join in the wartime spirit: SANDBAGS ON TOAST.

While Florence carried her gas mask in a simple cardboard case, more fashion-conscious people were determined to make a statement. They bought canvas or even leather cases. Some paid to have their initials applied in gold. Some women bought scarves to match their gas mask cases. Store mannequins displayed the latest stylish cases draped over their shoulders. And clothes manufacturers were beginning to design matching gas mask cases for outfits.

Some businesses tried to lighten the mood by decorating sandbags that lined their storefronts, painting them in pretty pastel blues, yellows, and pinks. At night taxis had to operate without headlights. Trips that had normally taken 5 minutes now took 20. On moonless nights the cities seemed "muffled in black velvet," and the large, dark buildings loomed as "huge caverns of inky shadow." People out for leisurely walks found themselves tripping over sandbags and bumping into trees in the darkened streets.

Some cities enforced sunset curfews, meaning people were supposed to stay home after the sun set. The government did not want large crowds to gather anywhere.

Store owners stacked sandbags in front of their stores in preparation for war. *University of Glasgow Archives & Special Collections, University collection, GB248 PHU72/1*

They would just tempt the enemy. Could any German pilot resist dropping a bomb or deadly chemicals on a big gathering of people? Many cinemas remained closed. Those that were open turned off the bright lights on their marquees. Sporting events were limited in size.

Meanwhile, Florence and Russell waited to hear from the US government. Surely a ship would arrive soon to take them back to their homes in America.

Within a few days word was sent to the American survivors. A ship called the *Orizaba* that was used as a mail carrier was on its way. It had been hired by the US

The *Orizaba*. *British Pathé*

government and outfitted with 400 cots. It would pick up the *Athenia* survivors in Europe and turn around for its return trip to America.

Some of the survivors were not happy with the news. They wanted the military to provide protection for them on the *Orizaba*. "We definitely refuse to go until we have a convoy," they told government officials. "You have seen what they will do to us."

But officials insisted the Germans would not attack a ship from the United States. After all, the two countries were not at war. They assured the survivors they would be safe. No convoy would travel with them.

"You can't trust the German government. You can't trust the German submarines," the survivors said.

Nonetheless, the *Orizaba* would set out from Glasgow on September 19, loaded with 150 American survivors of the *Athenia*, and sail into the Atlantic without military protection. Once again, Florence and Russell would embark on their journey home to Maple Heights and Philadelphia.

9

WELCOME HOME

"At least now I knew I wasn't an orphan." The news that his mom had been rescued and was back home in Philadelphia made Russell even more eager to return himself. He had many questions as he boarded the *Orizaba* on September 19 in Glasgow, Scotland. Most puzzling for the 11-year-old: Where was his dad?

Rebecca Park's return journey to the Park home in Philadelphia had been a nerve-racking, lonely voyage. From the time she was lifted out of her lifeboat on Monday, September 4, until her arrival at Market Street in Philadelphia on September 15, Russell's mom had lived through a nightmare. Separated from her husband and only child in the chaos of the explosion on the *Athenia*, she had endured a terrifying night in a lifeboat.

Returning to America in an uncomfortable, crowded freighter, she was tormented by uncertainty about the whereabouts of her family.

By the time she was reunited with Russell late in September, she had answers to some of her son's anxious questions. But others would never be answered. Some of the mysteries about the *Athenia* would never be solved. At least not for the Park family.

Rebecca had been rescued by the luxury yacht the *Southern Cross* in the early morning hours of Monday, September 4, after spending the night in a lifeboat. The beautiful craft was owned by a wealthy Swedish couple who were on their way to the Bahamas for a vacation when they heard the radio distress call from the *Athenia*.

"SOS from *Athenia* . . . sinking fast," read the radio call. The *Southern Cross* captain, James McClelland, sent a message back: "Full steam ahead to your assistance."

Rebecca was one of 376 people the *Southern Cross* rescued. However, they didn't stay on the yacht for long— about six hours. When they were given the choice of transferring to the British destroyer the *Escort* or to the American freighter, *City of Flint*, Russell's mom chose *City of Flint*, which would take survivors to the Canadian port of Halifax. She didn't know her son was on the *Escort*, heading back to Scotland.

The transfer from the yacht to the freighter was another stressful feat. Passengers had to get back into lifeboats. The Swedish crew carefully lowered the passengers one at a time down to other crewmen who caught them in the wobbling boats. They traveled a short distance between the *Southern Cross* and the *City of Flint*. Once again the crew helped the survivors climb up to the deck of the big ship.

The *City of Flint* had been headed from the United Kingdom to America when it, like the *Southern Cross*, heard the *Athenia's* distress call. In fact, although a freighter, it already carried some passengers who were fleeing Europe because of the war. So when they received the SOS, the passengers helped the crew prepare for the *Athenia* survivors. They knew the new arrivals would be hungry and cold, so they worked all night making sandwiches and vats of coffee.

The captain of the freighter, Joseph A. Gainard, had to hastily make changes to his ship when he learned it would be carrying over 200 passengers, which it was not equipped to do. Freighters normally carried products, not people. So the crew built bunks with strips of canvas fabric stretched over wooden frames. They stacked the beds three rows across and two beds high in the cargo hold.

When the survivors arrived on the *City of Flint*, they soon learned they would have to make sacrifices. There was very little privacy. Rebecca shared bunk space with other women. The canvas bunks had been lined with thick brown paper to keep the fabric clean. Whenever someone moved, the paper crinkled. Not everyone had blankets; but for those who did, it didn't take long for them to become coated with oil and dirt.

Rebecca and the other passengers cleaned themselves as best they could. Many, including Rebecca, were still covered with the slick oil from the explosion. They had to wait in line to use the washrooms. And there was a limited supply of freshwater and soap. There were few toothbrushes, so people shared.

The freighter's noises, especially at night, frightened the jittery survivors. The usual banging and clanging of a large freighter as it bounced on the seas was unnerving to the passengers. The screech of the ship's foghorn grated on nerves. The sounds of waves crashing against the sides of the vessel were terrifying to people who had just survived hours on the open water.

The rough seas caused the freighter, not designed for the comfort of passengers, to bounce and lurch day and night. Someone described the experience as "trying to sleep on a bucking bronc." It didn't help when the *City of Flint* encountered a big storm the first night after the *Athenia* survivors arrived on board. "I thought I'd die," one of the survivors said. "The freighter rocked horribly in the crashing waves."

Because the *City of Flint* had only about 30 passengers when it left the United Kingdom, the crew had planned meals accordingly. With the addition of the *Athenia* survivors, food was in short supply. But there were cereal, eggs, meat, soup, and fresh bread. And the evening meal offered meat, vegetables, and dessert. Meals were eaten in shifts. Because there were so many to be fed, diners were encouraged to limit their meals to 10 minutes.

One of the lowest points of the voyage was when passengers learned that little Margaret Hayworth, the Canadian girl who had been struck by a piece of wood on the night of the explosion, had died. She had passed in and out of consciousness throughout the journey. But on Saturday, September 9, the 10-year-old died. The crew cleared a cabin for her mother so she could mourn privately. The captain ordered the flag atop the *City of Flint* to fly at half-staff.

Although there was plenty of discomfort and sadness onboard the *City of Flint* during the 12-day journey, there were cheery and lighthearted times too. A birthday party, complete with a cake decorated with orange peels, was held for one of the children. The rows of flimsy bunks that had quickly been built by the crew became known by famous New York City landmarks: Times Square, Flatiron Building, and Park Avenue. Someone posted a list of rules, including one that read: "If you must be sick, for heaven's sake, lean over the rail." And one day the passengers watched whales performing off the starboard side of the ship.

Someone got the idea, after noticing all the unusual clothing the survivors were wearing, to have a fashion show. There was the little girl dressed in a lady's sunsuit, covered with a man's shirt. Another girl strutted in a sailor's uniform top with a towel wrapped around her waist as a skirt. A woman opened her fur coat to show off her pajamas underneath. Another little girl wore a pair of socks she'd gotten from one of the sailors; they were tied up above her knee with pieces of string. Other kids wore squares of canvas fabric as shoes, tied to their ankles with ropes.

The final night on the *City of Flint* was another violent time of pitching and rolling on the sea as the wind picked up. Many passengers were frightened again as they remembered the horrors of the night at sea in the lifeboats. But on September 13 the *City of Flint* pulled into Halifax, Nova Scotia, Canada. (The ship went to Halifax rather than its original destination of New York because the Canadian port was closer.) The passengers lined the rails, "many laughing, some weeping" as they shouted to the cheering crowds on shore.

Red-jacketed Royal Canadian Mounted Police stood rigidly at attention in honor of the survivors, and Red Cross nurses greeted them, offering food, clothes, and hot baths. The injured were taken to hospitals. John Hayworth, father of little Margaret who had died, embraced his wife as she stepped off the gangplank. The two clung to each other, sobbing as they made their way through the crowd.

One newspaper reported spotting a woman in an "oil-smeared kimono" standing apart from the crowd. "Her shoulders shook with sobs as she watched other passengers greeted by friends," the reporter wrote.

The woman was Rebecca Park. There were no family members or friends in Canada to greet her. The Red Cross arranged for her travel by train to the United States. She arrived at her house in Philadelphia on Friday,

September 15. At last she was home. Now she waited for the arrival of her son.

Meanwhile, Russell, Florence, and the other *Athenia* survivors stranded in Europe prepared to board the ship sent by the US government to take them home.

"The *Orizaba* really stood out in the harbor," Russell recalled.

"It was lit up like a cruise ship," Florence remarked.

The two were very impressed with the *Orizaba* as they stood in Glasgow harbor on Tuesday, September 19. While all the other ships in the harbor were painted "wartime gray" to help hide them from enemy planes and torpedoes, the *Orizaba* stood out because it was painted a bright white. And there were American flags painted on the sides and decks of the ship to make the Germans aware that the *Orizaba* was an American ship and should not be fired upon. The flags were intended to make everyone feel safe; the American government had faith that the Germans would not attack an American ship. "They figured Hitler did not want the United States in the war at that time," Florence explained.

But not all the passengers were convinced. Many were very worried about setting out onto the wide Atlantic Ocean again. And they were once again told by government officials that there would be no protection from a convoy. One survivor fretted, "I do hope we will be all right on this ship. I could not go through it a second time."

Maisie Levine was one of the survivors who was eager to board the *Orizaba* and return to her home

**Maisie Levine and her baby, Stephen, were rescued by sail-
ors who pulled the baby to safety in a bucket.** *International
News Photos*

in Brooklyn, New York. As she boarded the ship in
Glasgow with baby Stephen in her arms, she said good-
bye to her parents. After being rescued from the lifeboat,
Maisie and Stephen, who had been lifted to the *Escort* in

a pail, had stayed with her parents in Glasgow. Stephen had celebrated his first birthday only days before with his grandparents. He was too young to realize the dangers he and his mother faced as they began their second voyage home.

As the *Orizaba* moved out of the harbor at Glasgow, other boats tooted their whistles as a final farewell to the *Athenia* survivors. Florence remembered dockworkers shouting, "Good luck. Get home safe!"

Before heading into the waters of the Atlantic, the ship stopped at Galway, Ireland, to pick up about 90 survivors who had been staying there. On the evening of September 20, the *Orizaba* left Galway, continuing its voyage home to America.

Russell was surprised and pleased to see that one of the passengers who boarded at Galway was a Catholic priest whom he and his family had met on their voyage over to Ireland. Russell told the priest that he didn't know where his dad was. And he wondered how he would get home to Philadelphia when the *Orizaba* dropped anchor at the port in New York City. The two cities were about 100 miles apart. The priest assured Russell that he would help him get home if no one was in New York to meet him.

The ship was commanded by Captain A. M. Moore, a veteran sea captain, who always traveled with his two pets, a gray-colored cat named Fluff, and Hermann, his pet canary. Because it had been most recently in use as a mail carrier, the *Orizaba* was set up to transport bags and boxes. Before leaving America, it had been adapted for the *Athenia* survivors. The ship's sleeping quarters could hold only about 230 people, so carpenters had been put to work making the ship ready to hold almost 400 passengers. The swimming pool was covered over and lined with cots. Some said the long white rows of cots made the *Orizaba* "resemble a hospital ship."

As *Athenia* survivors arrived, they were assigned sleeping spots. Russell immediately realized the ship was "overflowing" with passengers. He was sent to a row of cots set up in an old lounge that had been converted to sleeping quarters. He shared the space with many others. Florence and Mary were lucky to have a cabin.

Some passengers were pleased with conditions on the rescue ship. "This is the most beautiful boat I have ever seen," one woman gushed. Another was not impressed. She said the *Orizaba* was "pretty unpleasant." But everyone agreed that they were happy to be heading home.

The *Orizaba* had been at sea for six days when on Sunday, September 24, the passengers were awakened in the middle of the night by sounds that spread fear and horror throughout the ship. Most thought they knew exactly what was happening, and they became hysterical. They feared it was another attack.

"We dashed from our berths and tried to get our life belts on. But we were so weak with fright, we couldn't get them on," a survivor recalled. "At first I thought it was an alarm clock, but it kept on ringing. Then we knew it was a submarine alarm!"

"It was panic city!" Florence recalled.

But the blasts that startled the passengers were a false alarm. There was a short in the ship's electrical system, causing the alarm to go off. The ship's crew scrambled to calm the passengers. Some were unable to handle the situation, and Rudolph Mueller, the ship's doctor, was called to treat several for hysteria.

Some passengers had been sleeping on the decks dressed in their clothes and wearing their life belts from the beginning of the voyage. They were too spooked to sleep belowdecks after their frightening experience on the *Athenia*. After the false alarm on the *Orizaba*, more stayed on top. When Florence suggested she and Mary do the same, Mary said, "No, we will sleep in our cabins whatever happens." She wanted to assure Florence that she was not afraid.

On Thursday, September 28, passengers lining the decks of the *Orizaba* shouted for their fellow passengers to look across the water. They pointed in awe as they spotted the Statue of Liberty through the mist of the "fine chilling rain" that fell over New York City. As the ship approached the harbor, "thousands" stood on the docks "in a wild salute" to her arrival. The sight of the city was breathtaking to the *Athenia* survivors.

The sounds were striking too. A newspaper reporter described the noise as the ship slowly moved to dock: "In an undertone to the roar of cheering and cries of greeting, there was the sound of weeping from the men, women, and children whose relatives were home safe at last."

As the passengers began to disembark, representatives from the American Express Company greeted them. They were present to give money to people who had lost all their money on the *Athenia*. They took the word of passengers who told the bank representatives how much they had lost. It was a relief to those who had wondered how they would travel from New York to

Rebecca and Russell Park were reunited in America. *Acme Photo*

their homes. But most passengers who made their way down the gangplank onto US soil weren't interested in the bank workers or their money.

Maisie and baby Stephen Levine disembarked at the pier at the foot of West 18th Street in Manhattan. "Amid a profusion of hugs, tears, and kisses" the two were welcomed home by their husband and father, Dr. Julius Levine.

Florence spotted her dad right away in the crowd. As she ran from the gangplank into her dad's arms she was "very excited," she later said. "I ran to him and hugged and hugged him. We were laughing and crying at one time. We were happy to be back as a family."

Russell spotted Rebecca in the crowd on the pier too and ran to her. Rebecca threw her arms around her son. "Where's dad?" Russell asked, looking up into his mother's eyes, where he saw tears.

"Daddy is gone," Rebecca said.

10

UNCOVERED SECRETS

When the German submarine *U-110*, under the command of Fritz-Julius Lemp, attacked four British freighters in the waters near Iceland on May 9, 1941, the British returned fire. Lemp dived to 300 feet below the surface in his new submarine. But it was not enough. Ten depth charges from British destroyers that had been traveling with the freighters brought the German submarine to the surface. The submarine was blown "almost out of the water" and was "riddled by shells" from the British attackers, according to historian Max Caulfield's account.

Thirty-four of the German submarine crew raised their arms in surrender. Two officers floundered in the water. One was the first watch officer; the other was his captain, Fritz-Julius Lemp. According to Caulfield, as the first officer swam toward his commander, he "observed with strong emotion" the face of his captain "suddenly vanish from the surface of the sea."

Florence couldn't hide her glee in a 2010 interview when she talked about the fate of Oberleutnant Fritz-Julius Lemp, the German submarine captain who had torpedoed the *Athenia*. "They got him!" she exclaimed. When he had attacked the *Athenia* on the evening of September 3, 1939, Lemp had broken international laws. And he had killed over 100 innocent men, women, and children. He had forever changed the lives of many, like Russell, who never saw his father again.

Oberleutnant Lemp's death, almost two years after the *Athenia* attack, had come about in a wartime sea battle with Britain, one of America's closest allies. It would be very difficult for those who had been affected by the *Athenia* tragedy to mourn the loss of Oberleutnant Lemp.

Florence, Russell, and most other Americans believed the commander and crew of the German submarine had sunk the *Athenia* and committed a grave wrong, but the Germans presented a very different picture of the events that occurred on the evening of the *Athenia*'s sinking. And all through the war years, from 1939 to 1945, no one knew with certainty exactly what had caused the explosion and sinking of the *Athenia*.

Why did so many jump to the conclusion that the ship had been attacked by a German submarine? Because Great Britain had declared war on Germany only a few hours before the attack. Everyone had worried about how the Germans would respond to the declaration. And the German navy had attacked a passenger liner before, the *Lusitania* in 1915. But there was more. Many survivors of the *Athenia* were absolutely certain they had seen a submarine in the waters around the liner at the time of the explosion:

"It was a German sub! They torpedoed us and then shelled us!"

"The sub opened fire on us!"

"I saw the sub come up. She was only a short distance from us. She let go a torpedo."

The *Athenia*'s Captain Cook told authorities, "There is no doubt about it, my ship was torpedoed."

Newspaper headlines around the world added to the frenzy: Nazi Sub Gave No Warning Before Torpedoing *Athenia* and U-boat Strikes! and British Ship Torpedoed!

Pollster George Gallup did a survey of Americans. He asked, "Do you believe the Germans sank the *Athenia*?" The results were clear: 60 percent voted yes, 9 percent voted no, and 31 percent voted no opinion.

The Germans heard about the sinking of the *Athenia* on radio news reports. When the German authorities heard that the world was blaming them for the incident, they quickly responded by denying any responsibility. They said they did not have submarines in the area of the Atlantic where the passenger liner had been traveling. Newspaper headlines proclaimed the Germans' response:

GERMANS DENY RESPONSIBILITY and GERMANS DENY TOR-
PEDOING and GERMANS DENY SINKING SHIP; BLAME BRITISH.

The Germans not only disputed playing any part in
the disaster but also accused Great Britain of attacking
its own passenger ship! "The *Athenia* was torpedoed by
the British, and they will not fool the world or the USA!"
the German officials said.

The German government issued statements saying
Great Britain had plotted to get the United States to join
the war on their side, sinking the *Athenia* and blaming
Germany because they thought the United States would
be likely to enter the war if they believed the ship had
been attacked by the Germans. If it were true, Great
Britain had committed a shocking act, killing its own
citizens as well as Americans in order to get the United
States to join the fight against Germany.

It would be more than two years after the *Athenia*
tragedy before the United States did enter the war on the
side of Great Britain. When that happened in December 1941, most people were no longer thinking about the
Athenia. Other terrible events had taken place, including
an attack on an American naval base in Pearl Harbor,
Hawaii.

It wasn't until after the war ended in 1945 that the
mysteries of the *Athenia* attack were unraveled and
revealed to the world. German war criminals revealed
the truth in sworn testimonies to an international court
at Nuremberg, Germany. They told a shocking tale of a
terrible mistake and a devious cover-up.

"Was für ein Durcheinander!" (What a mess!) Ober-leutnant Lemp had exclaimed when he realized he had attacked a passenger liner. The German was close enough to the sinking *Athenia* to see women and children jumping into lifeboats. One of the torpedoes he had ordered his crew to launch from *U-30* had hit its mark as he had planned. But the Germans relating the story at Nuremberg claimed Lemp thought he was attacking an enemy ship carrying war supplies or possibly troops. It had been wartime, after all, and it was his job to destroy the enemy. But it was against the law for him to attack a ship carrying passengers. Oberleutnant Lemp had known he was in trouble for his terrible mistake.

He had broken international laws. And he had done something that his commanding officers and high officials in the German government would be extremely upset about. German naval officers had been given very clear orders about obeying the laws governing naval operations in wartime. Attacking a passenger ship was not allowed. At this point, the German leader, Adolf Hitler, had been playing by the rules of warfare. (This had changed later in the war.)

Oberleutnant Lemp had known he had to tell his superior officers what had happened. He headed back to Germany to tell them in person. But first, he swore his crew to secrecy. No one was to tell anyone that they had torpedoed a passenger ship. At the Nuremberg Trials a statement by a crewmember named Adolf Schmidt was presented stating that he was forced by Lemp to sign a paper that read, "I . . . swear . . . that I shall erase from my memory all happenings of this day."

On September 27, 1939, a little over three weeks after he had committed the deadly attack, Lemp had arrived in the German harbor city of Wilhelmshaven, greeted by the "wheeling and screaming" of seagulls and a brass band. He had immediately asked to meet with his commanding officers. The highest officers in the German navy had listened to Lemp's story and decided to hide the truth from the world. The notes in the *U-30* logbook were changed. No record would exist to show that the submarine had attacked the *Athenia*.

The German government had continued to say that the British had attacked their own ship. They had even started an outrageous rumor that Winston Churchill, a high-ranking British official and future prime minister, had sunk the *Athenia* with a "bomb set off on a wireless signal" from a location in London.

Oberleutnant Lemp had continued to serve as a submarine commander. He had destroyed many British ships and was awarded some of Germany's highest honors for his service. By the time he died in the sea battle with the British destroyers in May 1941, he was considered a hero.

At the time of the Nuremberg Trials held after the war in 1945 and 1946, Fritz-Julius Lemp had been dead for years. But the superior officers whom he had met with to explain his actions during the *Athenia* tragedy were still living. They were on trial for committing war

crimes. The world had not forgotten the terrible tragedy of the sinking of the passenger liner during the first
hours of war. The British and Americans wanted to see
Germans convicted as "murderers" for the ruthlessness
they showed during the war.

**German officials were tried for war crimes at the Nuremberg Tri-
als in 1945 and 1946.** *National Archives photo no. 540127*

When they were asked about the events surrounding the *Athenia*, the officers, Grand Admirals Karl Doenitz and Erich Raeder, admitted Germany had torpedoed the passenger liner. Doenitz, who was described as "cold" and "aloof" during the trials, said it was a "regrettable mistake."

"I met Oberleutnant Lemp . . . and he told me at once that he thought he was responsible for the sinking of the *Athenia*," Doenitz testified.

Doenitz and Raeder explained that everyone had been sworn to secrecy after Lemp revealed his role in the sinking of the *Athenia*. But the two military men struggled to "sidestep responsibility" for the cover-up by blaming "political people." They said they were merely taking orders from high-ranking politicians in Hitler's government.

"I had no part whatsoever in the political events in which Hitler claimed that no U-boat had sunk the *Athenia*," Doenitz angrily proclaimed at the trials.

However, the court did not agree. Doenitz and Raeder were convicted of multiple war crimes. Doenitz was given a 10-year sentence, and Raeder was sentenced to life in prison.

The headlines in 1946 screamed the news: EXPLODE MYTH *ATHENIA* SUNK BY BRITISH and NUREMBERG TRIAL REVEALS NAZI SUB SANK *ATHENIA*. They claimed what many people had known all along was true. At last, after years of lies and denials by the Germans, the mystery of the *Athenia* was solved and revealed to the world.

Lemp (on left) and Doenitz (on right) covered up the *Athenia* **attack.** *Bundesarchiv, Bild 545974165/Photographer Rudolf Peter*

Florence had never believed the lies. She was certain that the Germans were responsible for the disaster. And she didn't think much of Lemp's excuse that he had mistakenly thought the *Athenia* carried military supplies. "They could have come on board to determine if we had ammunition," she said.

The news that the Germans had been responsible for the *Athenia* tragedy didn't provide Russell with the answers he most wanted. He never learned with absolute certainty what happened to his dad.

"We did afterwards hope that the end of World War II would find him in a German prison camp, or that some other explanation of his whereabouts would come to light," Russell said when, as an adult, he wrote about the events that took his dad from him.

"We are forced to assume he is gone. Unfortunately, only silence and the wide ocean remain."

EPILOGUE

~~~

"**H**appy anniversary, Mom!" On September 3 every year Florence Kelly Roseman gets a phone call from her daughter, Mary. The two talk about the day in 1939 when Florence almost lost her life. It's a day Florence's three grandchildren have heard about all their lives. And it's a day Florence's newborn great-grandchild will hear about when she is old enough to understand the terrifying ordeal Florence experienced when she was only 14 years old.

"You didn't know if you were going to live to 15, let alone 90!" Florence's granddaughter reminded her when she celebrated her 90th birthday in 2015. Florence didn't need to be reminded. She vividly remembered the fear and uncertainty of the nightmarish hours at sea in 1939. And she always appreciated the joys and even the heartaches of life—because of the traumatic experience of the tragedy.

"I've had a wonderful life," Florence says.

There are fewer and fewer survivors left to tell the story of the sinking of the *Athenia* during the first days of World War II. There were 1,418 passengers and crew on the liner when it was attacked by the German submarine. A total of 112 people were killed or never accounted for. And 1,306 passengers and crew survived.

Those still living who have memories of the terrible attack are now elderly. They were children or teens in 1939. Some have entered a time and place where they no longer can talk about their memories. And some who survived the attack have passed away after living full lives. Everyone who lived through the ordeal remembered it all their lives. They were never the same after they made history by becoming part of the attack on the *Athenia*.

FLORENCE KELLY ROSEMAN

One of the first things Florence did when she returned home to Ohio was to get together with her best friend, Eileen, and give her a big hug. She started 10th grade and went on to complete high school over the next three years, graduating in 1942. She completed business college and took a job as a secretary at a major company in Cleveland.

Florence met her husband, William Roseman, a World War II veteran, and married him in 1948. They were married for 45 years before he died in 1994. Their only child, Mary, was born in 1959. In 1962 Florence started a business as a wedding planner. And over the years, she gave close to 200 talks to schoolchildren and civic groups about her *Athenia* adventure. She retired at the age of 85.

Florence still has the dress she was wearing on the *Athenia* and the bell-bottom trousers that the British sailor gave her when she was lifted from the lifeboat. And she still has the gas mask that she got when she returned to Glasgow after being rescued. Along with those physical mementoes, Florence has kept very clear memories of the wartime disaster at sea that shaped her life forever.

RUSSELL A. PARK

Russell returned to his hometown of Philadelphia and continued his education, graduating from Dobbins Vocational-Technical High School. He joined the Army Air Corps and served as a mechanic. After his military service, Russell earned a degree in chemical engineering from Drexel University in Philadelphia in 1952.

Russell worked as a chemical engineer for the Firestone Tire & Rubber Company. He wrote technical articles for journals and textbooks and taught courses at seminars.

Although Russell's career led him into the science field, he always fed his love of history. He wrote a history of the Old Norriton Presbyterian Church, one of the oldest churches in America. He was a volunteer tour guide at the Valley Forge National Historical Park, where he drove a tour bus, giving him the opportunity to share his love of history with tourists. He also taught a history course at the Valley Forge Historical Society. He detailed his experiences on the *Athenia* in an article in the magazine *World War II* in 1989.

He never lost his fascination with ships and the sea. He was a lifelong member of the Navy League of the United States and the US Naval Institute.

Russell married and had two daughters. He died in Philadelphia in 1996.

STEPHEN LEVINE

One of the youngest survivors—the one-year-old who was lifted from the lifeboat in a bucket—returned to his home in Brooklyn, New York. He "romped and frol-icked" at the Levine family home on Sixth Avenue until starting school. Stephen went on to Dartmouth College and graduated from New York University School of Medicine in 1963. He served in the navy during the Vietnam War, stationed at the Philadelphia Naval Hospital. Later he started a private medical practice in Cherry Hill, New Jersey, and Philadelphia.

Stephen married Rhea Joy Cottler in 1960. She was a professor of anatomy and physiology. They had three children and five grandchildren. The family took vacations throughout the United States, as well as Europe, the Middle East, South Africa, and Australia. Rhea died in 2002.

Stephen retired to Florida and continues to travel with his companion, Dolores Lashkevich. They have taken a trip around the world by private jet, cruised to Antarctica through the Panama Canal, and played golf in New Zealand.

Stephen was too young to remember the frightening events of the *Athenia* attack, but his parents often told him of his harrowing rescue in a pail.

MARGARET HAYWORTH

Hundreds gathered on September 17, 1939, at St. Andrew's Presbyterian Church in Hamilton, Ontario, Canada, for the funeral of 10-year-old Margaret Hayworth, the girl who had been struck by a piece of wood on the night a torpedo hit and sank the *Athenia*. "We must have no hatred or bitterness toward anyone," the minister told the crowd. Government leaders, family, and friends gathered to honor the "first victim of the second Great War to be buried in Canadian soil."

Loudspeakers allowed the public who stood outside the church to hear the words. Flags flew at half-mast throughout the city. Floral wreaths filled the church. After the service, Margaret was laid to rest on a hillside overlooking Hamilton Bay.

Despite the minister's words, a government official did not disguise his bitterness when he laid blame for Margaret's death. In a speech, he said the "world's jury" had found Adolf Hitler "guilty of murder."

ACKNOWLEDGMENTS

Thank you to Lisa Reardon, my editor at Chicago Review Press, for her guidance throughout the writing and publishing process. My gratitude goes to Dr. Francis M. Carroll, author of *Athenia Torpedoed: The U-Boat Attack That Ignited the Battle of the Atlantic*, for his unique perspective and unsurpassed research. My thanks go to Dr. Chad Timm, associate professor of education at Simpson College in Indianola, Iowa, for his expertise as a history professional. The insight and perspective of history educator Janet Wills was invaluable to me.

My appreciation goes to Cathy Angel for her friendship since that fateful fall of 1970. And my thanks go to Joan Haack for her loyal friendship and unwavering support (always, but especially in fall 1970). Gratitude to Kathy Plank, a faithful friend and supporter. Thanks to Martha Chancellor for her translation guidance and unending help as a librarian and friend since March 1952. Words of encouragement from my longtime friend Mary Winkels Iverson motivated me. Phyl Hinton's friendship inspired me. Opinions of Ty and Sophia Mullenbach were much appreciated. Thank you to Aubrey Higgins-Brewer and Emma Prine for their valuable sixth-grade and eighth-grade reactions. A big thanks goes to Zack Miller for his always honest answers. Brooklyn and Bailey Miller compelled me to look at history through the eyes of an eight-year-old and a teen. And Emerson Brumm reminded me to include animal stories from the past.

And my sincere appreciation goes to Florence Kelly Roseman, who delighted me with her wonderful accounts of surviving the attack. Thank you to Lisa Park, who helped tell her father's story. And thanks to Dr. Stephen Levine for sharing his family story about his rescue in a bucket.

TIME LINE

~~~

June 1939: Florence arrives in Liverpool on *Athenia* to start her summer holiday

August 16, 1939: Russell arrives in United Kingdom on *Transylvania* for family vacation

September 2, 1939: *Athenia* leaves United Kingdom with passengers going to Canada and the United States

September 3, 1939: Great Britain declares war on Germany

September 3, 1939: Explosion occurs on *Athenia*

September 3–4, 1939: *Athenia* survivors spend night in lifeboats

September 4, 1939: Rescue ships pick up survivors

September 13, 1939: *City of Flint* arrives at Halifax, Nova Scotia, Canada

September 19, 1939: *Orizaba* leaves United Kingdom with *Athenia* survivors

September 27, 1939: *Orizaba* arrives in New York City carrying *Athenia* survivors

1945–46: Nuremberg trials

NOTES

~~~

PROLOGUE

"every wave is your enemy": "The Sinking of Athenia," video, Glasgow Museums on Vimeo, https://vimeo.com/channels/glasgowmuseums/53499555.

CHAPTER 1: A KID'S WORLD

People who had been at her house: Corpus Christi (TX) Caller-Times, "Stella Walsh Seeks Triple in Olympics," May 12, 1939.

"We must be hard-boiled": R.J.N., letter to the editor, "Disagrees," Oakland (CA) Tribune, May 4, 1939.

"I don't think we can afford": Middletown (NY) Times, "Aid Overhead Costs Target of Treasurer," May 4, 1939.

"one of the most heavily armed": Associated Press, "Hitler Proclaims Germany One of Most Heavily Armed Nations," East Liverpool (OH) Evening Review, May 1, 1939.

"not afraid of war"; "many weapons and very strong hearts": San Bernardino (CA) Daily Sun, "Il Duce Tells Italians He's Ready to Wait," April 1, 1939.

"We may have to fight": Circleville (OH) Herald, "Britain, France Stand beside Poland," May 1, 1939.

"the biggest defense program": Associated Press, "Congress Still Has Much to Do," *East Liverpool (OH) Evening Review*, May 1, 1939.

"I have seen war": Franklin D. Roosevelt, "Address at Chautauqua, N.Y.," August 14, 1936, www.presidency.ucsb.edu/ws/?pid =15097.

CHAPTER 2: WORLD AT THE BRINK OF WAR

As many as 30 million: "The Great Depression in Global Perspective," Digital History, 2016, www.digitalhistory.uh.edu/disp _textbook.cfm?smtID=2&psid=3433.

On every street corner spies: *Guardian* (Manchester), "I Came from Vienna," March 24, 1939.

The reasons given: *Guardian* (Manchester), "Russian Purge," November 24, 1938.

"mighty Soviet Power": *Guardian* (Manchester), "Soviet Sea Power," July 5, 1938.

"most powerful arms": *Guardian* (Manchester), "German Plans for Expansion," May 24, 1939.

"invincible strength": *Guardian* (Manchester), "German Plans for Expansion," May 24, 1939.

"Now small children hack": *Guardian* (Manchester), "Chinese Children Eating Twigs and Leaves," March 22, 1938.

"bombed, destroyed and ransacked": *Guardian* (Manchester), "Italian Vandals," April 27, 1939.

"our doorbell was rung": *Guardian* (Manchester), "I Came from Vienna," March 24, 1939.

CHAPTER 3: GREAT VALUE FOR
YOUR TRAVEL DOLLAR

"super flying boat"; "all the comforts of home"; "all metal": *Circleville (OH) Herald*, "Planes Hauling 300 May Start Ocean Flights," May 4, 1939.

"grandest ocean liner in the world"; "alive with beauty, energy and strength": "Our Story: A Trip Across Time," The Queen Mary, www.queenmary.com/history/our-story/.

"one of the world's most powerful icebreakers": Brooklyn Daily Eagle, "Quebec as King and Queen Will See It," April 2, 1939.

"excellent lines"; "most up-to-date"; "of the latest design"; "imposing appearance": "Transylvania," Grace's Guide to British Industrial History, April 10, 2015, www.gracesguide.co.uk/Transylvania.

"solid propellers": Brooklyn Daily Eagle, "Anchor Liner *Transylvania* to Be Reconditioned," April, 17, 1938.

"fireproof building of brick"; "streamlined"; "in every way": Brooklyn Daily Eagle, "Anchor Line Moves to New Pier Facilities," March 6, 1938.

"exercise every muscle in the body": Frank Reil, "Line on Liners," Brooklyn Daily Eagle, August 25, 1939.

"After school I liked"; "broad of beam"; "very strong"; "floating bookshop": Robert Emory Steele, "Pilots Pen and Ocean Greyhound," Brooklyn Daily Eagle, January 9, 1927.

"famous cuisine, personal service and entertainment"; "outstanding value in ocean travel"; "A great value for your travel dollar": Display ad for Donaldson Atlantic Line, Ottawa Journal, April 29, 1939.

where over 7,000 workers: Francis M. Carroll, Athenia Torpedoed: The U-Boat Attack That Ignited the Battle of the Atlantic (Annapolis, MD: Naval Institute, 2012), 16.

"novelty and a sense of adventure": Anchor-Donaldson Line brochure, November 1926.

watertight bulkheads and doors: Carroll, Athenia Torpedoed, 16.

"all the comforts of a first-class hotel": Display ad for Cunard Anchor-Donaldson Line to Glasgow, Winnipeg Tribune, March 22, 1926.

"pleasure and contentment": Display ad for Anchor-Donaldson Line, Ottawa Journal, April 8, 1925.

"quiet elegance": Florence Kelly Roseman, telephone interview by author, February 26, 2016.

Domed ceilings; marble columns: Max Caulfield, Tomorrow Never Came (New York: W. W. Norton, 1958), 41.

CHAPTER 4: FRANTIC ESCAPE

"in vacation mode": Kelly Roseman interview, January 9, 2016.

"It was a fabulous summer": Kelly Roseman interview, January 9, 2016.

"The fate of refugees": *Guardian* (Manchester), "A Case for Urgency," August 3, 1939.

"one of the most terrible of human problems": *Guardian* (Manchester), "Settlement of Refugees," August 5, 1939.

"You'd better try": Kelly Roseman interview, January 9, 2016.

"The situation has reached a point": *Guardian* (Manchester), "Another Day of Preparation," August 25, 1939.

"There are thousands ready": Cathleen Schurr, "Worst 36 Hours I Have Lived Through," *Brooklyn Daily Eagle*, September 16, 1939.

The 420 passengers: Carroll, *Athenia Torpedoed*, 20.

"drawn faces"; "pinched expressions": Schurr, "Worst 36 Hours."

136 passengers and refugees boarded: Carroll, *Athenia Torpedoed*, 21.

"The Athenia *did not have"; "dark as a tomb"*: Russell A. Park, "Aboard the *Athenia*," *World War II* 4 (July 1989): 34.

546 more passengers: Carroll, *Athenia Torpedoed*, 22.

As the liner embarked; That was 200 extra passengers: Carroll, *Athenia Torpedoed*, 22, 15.

"Others would give their lives": Schurr, "Worst 36 Hours."

CHAPTER 5: ATTACK AT SEA

"This morning the British Ambassador": Neville Chamberlain, "Declaration of War," September 3, 1939, www.bbc.co.uk/archive /ww2outbreak/7957.shtml?page=txt.

Fresh, gentle breezes swept: Donald A. Wilcox, "The *Athenia* Saga," Nova Scotia Archives, Nova Scotia, Canada, 2000.

"few places where they were not allowed": Park, "Aboard the *Athenia*," 36.

"the cleanest boy in the world": Park, "Aboard the *Athenia*," 36.

Lemp ordered his crew to submerge U-30: Carroll, *Athenia Torpedoed*, 30.

blasting a gaping hole: Thomas E. Finley, "US Survivor Describes Sinking of *Athenia*," *Brooklyn Daily Eagle*, September 5, 1939.

Lemp ordered the crew to return to the surface: Geirr H. Haarr, *The Gathering Storm: The Naval War in Northern Europe September 1939–April 1940* (Barnsley, UK: Seaforth, 2013), 80; Carroll, *Athenia Torpedoed*, 30.

The radio operator George Hoegell: "The Sinking of Athenia," video, Glasgow Museums on Vimeo, https://vimeo.com/channels /glasgowmuseums/53499555.

Witnesses said: Carroll, *Athenia Torpedoed*, 41.

"terrific explosion"; "rock from side to side": Florence Kelly Roseman, interview by Tom Vince, Hudson Cable TV, Hudson, Ohio, July 15, 2015.

"We were told to go": Kelly Roseman, interview by Vince, 2015.

"loud metallic bang": Park, "Aboard the *Athenia*," 36.

"very scared"; "Something's happened": Park, "Aboard the *Athenia*," 36.

"My first thought": Kelly Roseman, interview by Vince, 2015

"absolute carnage": Haarr, *The Gathering Storm*, 81.

"frightful screams": Finley, "US Survivor Describes."

"heavy powdery smell"; "parched"; "filled with a kind of fine soot": Schurr, "Worst 36 Hours."

"funny odor like gas": Ruby Mitchell Boersma, interview by Amber Lloydlangston, Canadian War Museum, Ottawa, Ontario, Canada, February 7, 2006.

"an ugly cloud of brown powder"; "like an evil eye": Schurr, "Worst 36 Hours."

"I could smell burning paint": Park, "Aboard the *Athenia*," 36.

"a burned bundle of rags": Park, "Aboard the *Athenia*," 37.

"staring vacantly into space": Schurr, "Worst 36 Hours."

"I stumbled over one man": Ian Johnston, "World War 2 Anniversary: The First Shot," *Telegraph* (London), September 2, 2009, www .telegraph.co.uk/history/world-war-two/6111620/World-War -2-anniversary-the-first-shot.html.

"I went up one deck"; "I went in and": *Brooklyn Daily Eagle*, "Boro Mother Tells How Baby 'Scared Stiff' Boarded Warship in Pail in *Athenia* Rescue," September 28, 1939.

Russell was alone: Russell is quoted in the *Idaho Falls Post-Register* describing his arrival in New York (William S. White, "Survivors Reach Home," September 28, 1939). He describes the situation slightly differently than he did in his 1989 article for *World War II* magazine. In the *Post-Register* Russell says he and his father went together to get his mother from her cabin and that he was separated from his parents when they went back to get their money from the cabin. In either case, Russell was separated from his parents and had to fend for himself.

"Oh, my gosh": Kelly Roseman, interview by Vince, 2015.

"This is the last one": Park, "Aboard the *Athenia*," 38.

We were on our own!: Park, "Aboard the *Athenia*," 38.

"It took a lot of courage": Park, "Aboard the *Athenia*," 37.

Before launching the final lifeboats through *"Abandon ship!":* Carroll, *Athenia Torpedoed,* 63.

CHAPTER 6: NIGHT OF TERROR

"All of us are sick now": Schurr, "Worst 36 Hours."

One boat was almost lowered: Carroll, *Athenia Torpedoed,* 65.

"Never shall I forget": Patricia Hale, "I Was on the *Athenia*," *Canadian Home Journal,* December 1939, 18.

"I saw one man gasp": *Milwaukee (WI) Journal,* "Horror Tales of *Athenia* Live On," September 13, 1939.

"ominous form"; "a silent shudder": Schurr, "Worst 36 Hours."

"Row, row": Hale, "I Was on the *Athenia*," 18.

"the vast nothingness": Schurr, "Worst 36 Hours."

"aged waiter"; "Row one, row two": Park, "Aboard the *Athenia*," 38.

"Nobody was panicky"; "Oh yes, they will": Kelly Roseman, interview by Vince, July 15, 2015.

"something unearthly about the whole scene": Schurr, "Worst 36 Hours."

"I didn't care": Johnston, "World War 2 Anniversary."

He wasn't sleeping: *Brooklyn Daily Eagle,* "Boro Mother Tells."

"No!": Park, "Aboard the *Athenia*," 39.

"eerie hulk": Schurr, "Worst 36 Hours."

"It was encouraging": Park, "Aboard the *Athenia*," 38.
"an eternity": Park, "Aboard the *Athenia*," 39.
"far-off Christmas trees": Caulfield, *Tomorrow Never Came*, 148.
"Soon we could see": Hale, "I Was on the *Athenia*," 28.
"This ship kept coming": Johnston, "World War 2 Anniversary."

CHAPTER 7: INCREDIBLE RESCUE

"We were aware of large dark shapes": Park, "Aboard the *Athenia*," 39.
"We realized they": Kelly Roseman, interview by Vince, July 15, 2015.
"It's no use!"; "Come on, come on"; "Come on, let's go": Schurr, "Worst 36 Hours."
"They raised my baby": *Brooklyn Daily Eagle*, "Boro Mother Tells."
"Oh, it was wonderful": Kelly Roseman, interview by Vince, July 15, 2015.
"into many helping hands": Park, "Aboard the *Athenia*," 39.
"Frenzied screams"; "brief night shirt"; "Geoffrey, Geoffrey!"; "Here I am, Mom": Schurr, "Worst 36 Hours."
Not long after this another mishap: Haarr, *The Gathering Storm*, 84.
One very lucky boy: Hale, "I Was on the *Athenia*," 29.
"She's going down": Park, "Aboard the *Athenia*," 39.
"suddenly all that was left of her disappeared": Hale, "I Was on the *Athenia*," 29.
Luckily not long before: Carroll, *Athenia Torpedoed*, 81.
"large white yacht": Park, "Aboard the *Athenia*," 40.

CHAPTER 8: THE WAIT

"We were afraid Hitler": Kelly Roseman, interview by Vince, July 15, 2015.
The Electra carried 238 Athenia survivors; the Escort, 402: Carroll, *Athenia Torpedoed*, 159.
Scotland's finest hotels: Park, "Aboard the *Athenia*," 40.
the 430 people who had been rescued by the Knute Nelson: Carroll, *Athenia Torpedoed*, 159; Francis M. Carroll, "'The First Casualty of the Sea': The *Athenia* Survivors and the Galway Relief Effort,

September 1939," *History Ireland* 19 (Jan./Feb. 2011), www
.historyireland.com/20th-century-contemporary-history
/the-first-casualty-of-the-sea-the-athenia-survivors-and-the
-galway-relief-effort-september-1939/.

About midnight, Harry; "adopted"; "I was in tears": Kelly Roseman
interview, January 9, 2016.

"a terrifying experience": Park, "Aboard the *Athenia*," 41.

"SHOP IN SAFETY, SHELTER AVAILABLE" through *"huge caverns of inky
shadow"*: *Observer* (Manchester), "The Life of the Nation," September 17, 1939.

"We definitely refuse"; "You can't trust"; the Orizaba would set out:
Guardian (Manchester), "Survivors of *Athenia*," September 8, 1939.

CHAPTER 9: WELCOME HOME

"At least now I knew I wasn't an orphan": Lisa Park, telephone interview by author, March 7, 2016.

"SOS from Athenia . . . sinking fast"; "Full steam ahead to your assistance.": Richard Savill, "Chilling Telegram Tells of First British Ship to Be Sunk in Second World War," *Telegraph* (London), February 5, 2009, www.telegraph.co.uk/news/uknews/4524670/Chilling-telegram-tells-of-first-British-ship-to-be-sunk-in-Second-World-War.html.

376 people the Southern Cross: Carroll, *Athenia Torpedoed*, 159.

The freighter's noises, especially at night: Hale, "I Was on the *Athenia*," 30.

"trying to sleep on a bucking bronc": *Corvallis (OR) Daily Gazette-Times*, "William Welch, Local Man Enroute Home from Europe on *Athenia* Rescue Ship, Writes Detail," September 20, 1939.

"I thought I'd die": Daniel Francis, "Dorothy's War: The Sinking of the *Athenia*," Reading the National Narrative, April 1, 2006, www.danielfrancis.ca/content/sinking-athenia.

the City of Flint *had only about 30 passengers*: Carroll, *Athenia Torpedoed*, 11.

But there were cereal, eggs: Carroll, *Athenia Torpedoed*, 105.

Meals were eaten in shifts: Hale, "I Was on the *Athenia*," 30.

"If you must be sick": Hale, "I Was on the *Athenia*," 31.

"many laughing, some weeping": United Press, "200 of *Athenia* Survivors Land," *Harrisburg (PA) Evening News*, September 13, 1939.

"oil-smeared kimono"; "Her shoulders shook": Gardner Frost, "Passengers from *Athenia* Verify Torpedo Stories," *Dunkirk (NY) Evening Observer*, September 13, 1939.

"The Orizaba *really"*: Park, "Aboard the *Athenia*," 41.

"It was lit up": Debbie Hanson, "Florence Kelly Roseman Survived a 'Night of Terror,'" clevelandwomen.com, 2010, www.clevelandwomen.com/people/florence-kelly-rosman.htm.

"wartime gray": Park, "Aboard the *Athenia*," 41.

"They figured Hitler": Hanson, "Florence Kelly Roseman."

"I do hope we will": *Indiana (PA) Evening Gazette*, "Athenians Sail for Home," September 19, 1939.

"Good luck": Kelly Roseman, interview by Vince, July 15, 2015.

"resemble a hospital ship": White, "Survivors Reach Home."

"overflowing": Park, "Aboard the *Athenia*," 41.

"This is the most beautiful boat": Henrietta S. Hill, "Miss Jeanette Jordan, Rescued from Torpedoed 'Athenia,' Reaches Home," *Freeport (IL) Journal-Standard*, October 5, 1939.

"pretty unpleasant": *Brooklyn Daily Eagle*, "*Athenia*'s Heroine," October 1, 1939.

"We dashed from our berths"; "At first I thought it was": *Bakersfield Californian*, "Mrs. Howe Tells *Athenia* Ordeal," October 4, 1939.

"It was panic city!"; "No, we will sleep in our cabins": Kelly Roseman interview, January 9, 2016.

"fine chilling rain," through *In an undertone to the roar*: *York (PA) Gazette and Daily*, "240 S.S. *Athenia* Survivors Arrive," September 28, 1939.

As the passengers began to disembark: *Kingston (NY) Daily Freeman*, "*Athenia* Survivors Reach New York," September 28, 1939.

"Amid a profusion of hugs": *Brooklyn Daily Eagle*, "Boro Mother Tells."

"very excited"; "I ran to him": Kelly Roseman interview, January 9, 2016.

"Where's dad": Coshocton (OH) Tribune, "240 More *Athenia* Survivors Arrive in United States," September 28, 1939.

"Daddy is gone": Park, "Aboard the *Athenia*," 41.

CHAPTER 10: UNCOVERED SECRETS

"almost out of the water"; "riddled by shells"; "observed with strong emotion"; "suddenly vanish from the surface of the sea": Max Caulfield, *"Athenia* Sinking 'Churchill Plot' Said Germans," *Age* (Melbourne), November 24, 1958.

"They got him!": Hanson, "Florence Kelly Roseman."

"It was a German sub!"; "The sub opened fire on us"; "I saw the sub come up": United Press, "200 of *Athenia* Survivors Land."

"There is no doubt about it": Carroll, *Athenia Torpedoed*, 117.

NAZI SUB GAVE NO WARNING; U-BOAT STRIKES!: Winnipeg (MB) Tribune, September 4, 1939.

BRITISH SHIP TORPEDOED!: Helena (MT) Independent Record, September 3, 1939.

Pollster George Gallup: Dr. George Gallup, "Study Reveals Awareness of Propaganda," *Salt Lake (UT) Tribune*, September 28, 1939.

GERMANS DENY RESPONSIBILITY: Abilene (TX) Reporter News, September 4, 1939.

GERMANS DENY TORPEDOING: Salem (OR) Daily Capital Journal, September 4, 1939.

GERMANS DENY SINKING SHIP; BLAME BRITISH: Nevada State Journal (Reno, NV), September 5, 1939.

"The Athenia *was torpedoed by the British"*: International Military Trials, Nazi Conspiracy and Aggression, Supplement A, US Government Printing Office, 1947: 1065

"Was für ein Durcheinander!": Carroll, *Athenia Torpedoed*, 31; Caulfield, *Tomorrow Never Came*, 67.

"I . . . swear . . . that I shall erase": "Erich Raeder," *Nazi Conspiracy and Aggression*, vol. 2, chapter 16, part 15, Avalon Project, Yale

Law   School,   http://avalon.law.yale.edu/imt/chap16_part15
.asp.

On September 27, 1939, a little over: Carroll, *Athenia Torpedoed*, 131;
Harrisburg *(PA) Telegraph*, "Doenitz Explodes Myth That British Sank Own Liner," January 15, 1946.

"wheeling and screaming": Caulfield, *"Athenia* Sinking."

The German government had continued: Danville *(VA) Bee*, "Who Sank
the *Athenia?"* May 22, 1946.

"murderers": James F. King, "Disclose Nazis Sank *Athenia,"* Alton
(IL) Evening Telegraph, January 15, 1946.

"cold"; "aloof": James F. King, "Explode Myth *Athenia* Sunk by British," Freeport *(IL) Journal Standard*, January 15, 1946.

"regrettable mistake": Danville *(VA) Bee*, "Who Sank the *Athenia?"*

"I met Oberleutnant Lemp": William L. Shirer, *The Rise and Fall of
the Third Reich: A History of Nazi Germany* (New York: Simon &
Schuster, 1959), 637.

"sidestep responsibility"; "political people": Brooklyn *Daily Eagle*, *"Athenia* Sinking Honest Mistake Doenitz Claims," May 10, 1946.

"I had no part whatsoever": King, "Explode Myth *Athenia."*

EXPLODE MYTH ATHENIA SUNK BY BRITISH: King, Freeport *(IL) Journal
Standard.*

NUREMBERG TRIAL REVEALS NAZI SUB SANK ATHENIA: Monroe *(WI) Evening Times*, January 15, 1946.

"They could have come on board": Hanson, "Florence Kelly Roseman."

what happened to his dad: Rebecca Park said upon her return to
the United States that a woman on the *Athenia* told her she
had seen Alexander "killed by the explosion" (Gardner Frost,
"Athenia Survivors Land in Halifax; Give Accounts of Terror
as Torpedo Struck," Valparaiso *(IN) Vidette-Messenger*, September 13, 1939). Russell never mentioned this in his magazine
account of the sinking of the *Athenia* as an adult. Was the
newspaper account inaccurate? If it was accurate, did Russell's
mother ever tell him about the woman? Did Rebecca doubt
the woman's story? That would seem to be the case in view of
Russell's statements in the magazine article about never learn-
ing with certainty what happened to his father.

"We did afterwards hope"; "We are forced": Park, "Aboard the Athenia," 41.

EPILOGUE

"Happy anniversary, Mom!"; "You didn't know": Kelly Roseman,
interview by Vince, July 15, 2015.
"I've had a wonderful life": Kelly Roseman interview, February 16,
2016.
"romped and frolicked": Brooklyn Daily Eagle, "Boro Mother Tells."
"We must have no hatred"; "first victim of the Second": Ottawa (ON)
Journal, "Grave of Child is Canadians' Rallying Point," September 18, 1939.
"world's jury"; "guilty of murder": Brooklyn Daily Eagle, "Ask Flags at
Half Mast for Athenia Victim," September 15, 1939.

BIBLIOGRAPHY

BOOKS

Carroll, Francis M. *Athenia Torpedoed: The U-Boat Attack That Ignited the Battle of the Atlantic.* Annapolis, MD: Naval Institute, 2012.

Caulfield, Max. *Tomorrow Never Came.* New York: W. W. Norton, 1958.

Deverell, William, and Deborah Gray White. *United States History.* Orlando, FL: Holt McDougal, 2012.

Haarr, Geirr H. *The Gathering Storm: The Naval War in Northern Europe September 1939–April 1940.* Barnsley, UK: Seaforth, 2013.

MEMOIRS

Hale, Patricia. "I Was on the *Athenia.*" *Canadian Home Journal,* December 1939.

Stewart, D. G. B. "Homeward Bound on the *Athenia.*" *Canadian Banker,* October 1939.

Wilcox, Donald A. "The *Athenia* Saga." Nova Scotia Archives, Nova Scotia, Canada, 2000.

NEWSPAPER AND MAGAZINE ARTICLES

Brooklyn Daily Eagle. "Boro Mother Tells How Baby 'Scared Stiff' Boarded Warship in Pail in *Athenia* Rescue." September 28, 1939.

Danville (VA) Bee. "Who Sank the *Athenia*?" May 22, 1946.

Finley, Thomas E. "US Survivor Describes Sinking of Athenia." *Brooklyn Daily Eagle,* September 5, 1939.

Guardian (Manchester). "German Plans for Expansion." May 24, 1939.

Guardian (Manchester). "I Came from Vienna." March 24, 1939.

Hale, Patricia. "I Was on the *Athenia.*" *Canadian Home Journal,* December 1939, 8–9, 18, 28–31, 66.

Johnston, Ian. "World War 2 Anniversary: The First Shot." *Telegraph* (London), September 2, 2009. www.telegraph.co.uk /history/world-war-two/6111620/World-War-2-anniversary -the-first-shot.html.

King, James F. "Explode Myth *Athenia* Sunk by British." *Freeport (IL) Journal Standard,* January 15, 1946.

Park, Russell A. "Aboard the *Athenia.*" *World War II* 4 (July 1989): 34–41.

Schurr, Cathleen. "Worst 36 Hours I Have Lived Through." *Brooklyn Daily Eagle.* September 16, 1939.

United Press. "200 of *Athenia* Survivors Land." *Harrisburg (PA) Evening News,* September 13, 1939.

White, William S. "Survivors Reach Home." *Idaho Falls Post-Register,* September, 28, 1939.

SPEECHES

Chamberlain, Neville. "Declaration of War," September 3, 1939. www.bbc.co.uk/archive/ww2outbreak/7957.shtml?page=txt.

Roosevelt, Franklin D. "Address at Chautauqua." August 14, 1936. www.presidency.ucsb.edu/ws/?pid=15097.

REPORTS

"Erich Raeder." *Nazi Conspiracy and Aggression.* Vol. 2, chapter 16, part 15. Avalon Project. Yale Law School. http://avalon.law.yale .edu/imt/chap16_part15.asp.

International Military Trials, Nazi Conspiracy and Aggression, Supplement A, US Government Printing Office, 1947: 1065.

INTERVIEWS

Boersma, Ruby Mitchell. Interview by Amber Lloydlangston. Canadian War Museum, Ottawa, Ontario, Canada, February 7, 2006.

Boersman, Ruby Mitchell. Telephone interview by author. March 7, 2016.

Kelly Roseman, Florence. "Survivor of the WW II Torpedo Attack on the SS *Athenia* September 3, 1939." Interview by Tom Vince. Hudson Cable TV. Hudson, OH. July 15, 2015.

Kelly Roseman, Florence. Telephone interviews by author. January 9, 2016; February 26, 2016; March 12, 2016.

Levine, Stephen. Telephone interview by author. December 14, 2015.

Park, Lisa. Telephone interview by author. March 7, 2016.

VIDEOS

"8 Bells Lecture | Francis Carroll: Athenia Torpedoed." YouTube video. 58:25. Posted by "usnavalwarcollege." September 20, 2013. www.youtube.com/watch?v=sHk2CGkgBGw.

British Movietone Digital Archive. www.movietone.com.

British Pathé. www.britishpathe.com.

"The Sinking of Athenia." Video. Glasgow Museums on Vimeo. https://vimeo.com/channels/glasgowmuseums/53499555.

WEBSITES

Carroll, Francis M. "'The First Casualty of the Sea': The *Athenia* Survivors and the Galway Relief Effort, September 1939."

History Ireland 19 (Jan./Feb. 2011). www.historyireland.com/20th
-century-contemporary-history/the-first-casualty-of-the-sea-the
-athenia-survivors-and-the-galway-relief-effort-september-1939/.

Francis, Daniel. "Dorothy's War: The Sinking of the *Athenia*."
Daniel Francis: Reading the National Narrative. April 1, 2006.
www.danielfrancis.ca/content/sinking-athenia.

"The Great Depression in Global Perspective." Digital History.
2016. www.digitalhistory.uh.edu/disp_textbook.cfm?smtID=2
&psid=3433.

Gregory, Mackenzie J. Ahoy-Mac's Web Log. www.ahoy.tk-jk.net/.

Hanson, Debbie. "Florence Kelly Roseman Survived a 'Night of
Terror.'" clevelandwomen.com. 2010. www.clevelandwomen
.com/people/florence-kelly-rosman.htm.

"Our Story: A Trip Across Time." The Queen Mary. www.queen
mary.com/history/our-story/.

Saturday Evening Post. Display ad for Pan American. http://cruise
linehistory.com/wp-content/uploads/2011/09/PAA3.jpg.

"Transylvania." Grace's Guide to British Industrial History. April
10, 2015. www.gracesguide.co.uk/Transylvania.

INDEX

~~~

Page numbers in *italics*
indicate pictures.

A

air raid drills, 97
air travel, 21–23
Albania, 17
American Express, 114
animals, 35–36, 41
Athenia (ship), 26, *45*
    atmosphere, 30–33, *32*, *59*
    disaster, vii–xi, 54–58,
       118–121
    German cover-up, 118–126
    lifeboat drills, 50, 53
    lifeboats, *51*, 63–66
    overcrowding, 44–46
    sinking of, 71, 83
    travel route, 42–44, *43*, 49

war precautions, 44, 49–50
    See also survivors
Austria, 14, 17–18

B

Beresford Hotel, 91–93, *92*
blackouts, 98
Bone, David, 29
books, 4–5
Buchanan Arms Inn, 95

C

California (ship), 41–42
Cameron family, 96
Chamberlain, Neville, 52
China, 16, 17
Churchill, Winston, 122
City of Flint (ship), *85*

Athenia disaster, 58, 60
in Ireland, 37–38
previous travels, 23–24
rescue, 96, 104
return home, 103–104,
108–109
return tickets, 41–42
reunion with son, 114, 115
separation from son, 60, 84
travel plans, 3, 24–25
Park, Russell
aboard lifeboat, 67–68
aboard the *Athenia*, 53
aboard the *Escort*, 83
aboard the *Orizaba*, 103,
109, 111
aboard the *Transylvania*,
28, 34
Athenia disaster, viii, 56
background, 3
boarding lifeboat, 58, 60–61
boarding rescue boats, 80
on disappearance of father,
126
in Ireland, 37–38
later life, 129–130
observations about *Athenia*,
44
previous travels, 23–24
return tickets, 41–42
reunion with mother, 114,
115
in Scotland, 91–92, 96–97
travel plans, 3, 8, 24–25
Philadelphia, Pennsylvania, 5

Philadelphia Naval Shipyard,
5, 6
Poland, Nazi invasion, 19, 36,
42, 52

Q

Queen Mary (ship), 23–24

R

Raeder, Erich, 124
refugees, 6–7, 39
rescue disasters, 81
Roosevelt, Franklin D., 8
Roseman, Mary, 127, 128
Roseman, William, 128

S

sandbags, 99
Saurel (ship), 25
Schmidt, Adolf, 121–122
sea travel, 23–24
seasickness, 63, 64
shipyards, 5–6, 6
Shuster, Joe, 1
Siegel, Jerry, 1
Southern Cross (ship)
Athenia rescue, 76
rescue disasters, 81
transfers from, 84, 86,
104–105
Soviet Union, 12, 14, 16
spies, 14

El Problema
Con Los Secretos

por Karen Johnsen
ilustraciones por Linda Forssell